No Longer I

ENDORSEMENTS

"THIS BOOK IS FILLED WITH gospel power and biblical soundness. Jaska does not use his testimony for personal glory, like so many others, but instead uses it to point people to the One Who deserves all the glory, Jesus Christ. This book will convict and encourage you, as it conveys biblical truth in a clear and compelling way. Theologically sound, well-written, and inspiring! I highly recommend this book."

—DR. JOSHUA WEST
Evangelistic Preaching Voice and Executive Director
World Challenge, Inc.

"JASKA WAS RAISED IN A very religious home in Nepal surrounded by man-made gods. By not finding peace in the gods and having a fear of death, Jaska heard God speak to him through a dream with the simple words, 'Read the Bible.' That was the beginning of a relationship with God through His Son Jesus Christ. Filled with the power of the Holy Spirit, Jaska began a journey from Australia to America, where he has challenged believers to share the gospel. As a believer of sixty-plus years, his book has challenged me and will challenge you to lead people to the living God."

—DALTON CURRIE
Pastor, Evergreen Baptist Church
Coldspring, Texas

A Journey From Hinduism to Christianity

No Longer I

LIVING FOR CHRIST

AND HIS GOSPEL

JASKA
DUWADI

AMBASSADOR INTERNATIONAL
GREENVILLE, SOUTH CAROLINA & BELFAST, NORTHERN IRELAND

www.ambassador-international.com

No Longer I

Living for Christ and His Gospel

©2025 by Jaska Duwadi
All rights reserved

ISBN: 978-1-64960-883-3, hardcover
ISBN: 978-1-64960-636-5, paperback
eISBN: 978-1-64960-685-3

Edited by Lauren Cleveland
Cover Design by Hannah Linder Designs
Interior Typesetting by Dentelle Design

This work depicts actual events in the life of the author as truthfully as recollection permits. While all persons and stories within are real, names and identifying characteristics have been changed to respect their privacy.

All Scripture quotations are taken from the The ESV® Bible (The Holy Bible, English Standard Version®), © 2001 by Crossway, a publishing ministry of Good News Publishers. ESV Text Edition: 2025.

AMBASSADOR INTERNATIONAL
Emerald House
411 University Ridge, Suite B14
Greenville, SC 29601
United States
www.ambassador-international.com

AMBASSADOR BOOKS
The Mount
2 Woodstock Link
Belfast, BT6 8DD
Northern Ireland, United Kingdom
www.ambassadormedia.co.uk

The colophon is a trademark of Ambassador, a Christian publishing company.

To all the beloved missionaries who choose to remain unknown yet labor tirelessly with blood, sweat, and tears to advance the blessed gospel in the world.

TABLE OF CONTENTS

INTRODUCTION

IN A TIME WHEN HUMANITY is fixated on self-advancement and anxiety is at an all-time high, mankind needs hope. Despite her self-proclaimed vision and power, the Church still struggles to influence the world to turn to the Lord, even during these dark and pressing times. The world's population urgently needs true conversion to Christ. Such a profound transformation of the soul ignites a fervent devotion to the Lord that remains steadfast in the face of temptation and adversity. Authentic conversion also inspires individuals to pursue revival, a necessity that our contemporary churches urgently require.

Life on earth is fleeting, and time slips away faster than we realize. Therefore, the main objective of this book is to present the reader with the reality of eternity and the realization that they will soon be standing before the judgment seat of Christ (2 Cor. 5:10). The heartbeat of this book is the salvation of the lost.

The life that preceded the fiery zeal to propagate the gospel of our blessed Lord is one that I am ashamed to speak about had it not been for the Lord's saving grace enabling me to declare it for the glory of His name. I was not privileged like the many Americans to have been raised in a Christian household. Being brought up in Kathmandu, Nepal, where we had no shortage of deities to worship, my interest in the afterlife began gradually after witnessing innumerable bloody animal sacrifices offered to the terrifying statues of various gods and goddesses. These rituals and others were performed with intense vigor and dedication by worshipers of the many

Hindu deities. Still, these gods and goddesses offered empty and unfulfilled promises of the future for their worshipers, so I was lost and without hope. I searched throughout my youth for answers to my questions about how I could be rescued from the horrors of death.

The desire to be freed from the power of death continued to torment me for a long time. I constantly sought deliverance from my anxious thoughts about what came after life's final breath. Thankfully, I was led, at last, to the Christ of Golgotha. Having experienced the mercy of the One Who sacrificed Himself to free me from the shackles of sin and death, I dedicated my unwavering loyalty to the Savior Who gave everything for me so that I could embrace all of Him. For once in my life, I felt safe in the loving arms of my Rescuer, Jesus Christ, the Savior and Hope of the world.

Jesus Christ, and Him alone, is Whom I want to glorify within the pages of this book. The message within comes from a heart heavily burdened over the lukewarm state of the Church that is too ashamed to preach and live the faith of the cross. This reluctance is a shameful disservice to a world unapologetically embracing and even celebrating sin. It is heartbreaking to see individuals who identify as members of the church engaging in sinful lifestyle that stand in stark contrast to the teachings of the Bible. This not only undermines their faith but also serves as a grave offense to the Holy God. Yet let us be clear: God will not tolerate mockery. Still, the Lord shows patience, much like a caring father waiting for his lost son to come home. God is waiting for sinners to turn back to Him, call on His name, and find salvation. Therefore, my prayer is for a change in the heart of the reader, especially those who may resist these words yet undoubtedly need them.

In this book, I have greatly emphasized topics such as sin, holiness, and repentance. It aims to leave you broken but not without hope, as the brokenness unveils the profound offerings of the cross of Calvary for a penitent soul. My words are crafted with the purpose of dethroning the proud from their pursuit of ungodly passions and adorning the humble with God's vision. The reading will end at some point, but the call for self-examination and response will live on.

My writing is supremely motivated by loyalty to God, with the ultimate goal of seeking His approval above all. I encourage readers to adopt a similar approach. Given the nature of this book, I am aware that its content may elicit either acceptance or complete rejection. Moreover, my personal view or a particularly stern Scripture will cause disagreements in some instances. When that happens, I ask the reader to weigh the content in light of the Scriptures.

To the believer, I pray these words add more fuel to the fire already kindled by the Holy Spirit. And to the slumbering child, I pray the words of this book will bring about a burning conviction of sin, leading to godly repentance and returning you to the love you had at first.

Finally, if you are an alien to the gospel, may the reading bring you nearer to the foot of the cross in faith and repentance. My hope is that your precious and curious souls will encounter the loving Jesus Christ within the pages of this book and that He will become your foundation in life from that moment forward, all for the glory of the Lamb. Amen.

For *"everyone who calls on the name of the Lord will be saved"* (Rom. 10:13).

CHAPTER 1
NEW CREATION

"To open their eyes, so that they may turn from darkness to light and from the power of Satan to God, that they may receive forgiveness of sins and a place among those who are sanctified by faith in me."

Acts 26:18

GROWING UP IN KATHMANDU, NEPAL, came with attachments to caste systems that dictated one's way of life and religion. It was a place where caste, rather than character, categorizes a person—an unfair system for an unfair place. I was raised in what some would call the highest and most sacred caste in Nepal, a Brahmin Bahun. The Brahmins were known to be of priestly descent. They were entrusted with all the religious duties relating to the temple with all its customs and rituals.

My family followed the Hindu faith, and my father, in particular, was very devoted to his religion. He visited the Hindu temple at least once a week on Saturdays, and I was asked to accompany him. I recall having strange and thought-provoking questions during those times, when I was around five or six years of age—questions like, "Why were the animals being killed?" "Why was their blood being sprinkled on these terrifying deities?" and "Why were there so many people standing in line to get a blessing from such horrific-looking statues?"

Each time I visited the temple, these questions were constantly circulating in my mind. I truly wondered if the people who visited the temple from near and far trusted these deities to bring them blessings in life. The sheer image of these statues—with their tongues sticking out, their glaring eyes, and the pitchforks they carried—were too dreadful for me to even look at, let alone worship. Why these grotesque, monstrous beings were so cherished was beyond me.

Concerning the deities themselves, there were different levels. Some deities, for example, were approachable. A layman could walk right in and submit himself before one in worship, but some were beyond the grasp of men due to their overly holy nature. Thus, the priests were to mediate between the sacred and the common. The most revered god that my family served was Ganesha, an elephant-headed Hindu god of knowledge, wisdom, intelligence, and prosperity. The statue of this particular god was found throughout my family's household.

Within my parent's household, the wall was a temple that was a real sight to behold. It was full of the idols of innumerable deities, such as Krishna, Ganesha, Kali, Saraswati, and many others. My family worshiped all these deities to better their spiritual lives and material blessings but to no avail, as the gods and goddesses failed. The reality was that things were not good in my family.

Death became a common reoccurrence in the family; and unlike the Hindu caste system, death showed no partiality and claimed whomever it pleased. Tragically, to my dismay, one of my beloved uncles, who cared for me with such tender affection, was swallowed up by it. When tragedies like this struck, hopelessness was always around the corner. It befriended the teary-eyed mourners and those who offered countless prayers to their gods. Additionally, after the passing of a loved one, the family priest held a ceremony in remembrance of the dead, known as the death anniversary.

This ritual would then go on to be performed every year in honor of the dead. During this time, some participants would abstain from certain foods and drinks. *But for what?* I would wonder. While many were mourning for the temporal, I was searching for answers for the eternal realm. Death had become a reality for me, and there was no avoiding or escaping it. My heart longed to know the meaning and purpose of life because the sudden thought of dying and ceasing to exist paralyzed me with fear.

I was often sick as a child and, at times, bedridden for days. This frequently happened with countless trips to clinics; and even a witch doctor believed, on certain occasions, I was under the influence of demonic possession. I could handle injections and all sorts of bitter medicines, but I dreaded going to the witch doctor. His house was always dark, with some candlelight accompanied by a putrid odor. With a straw broom in his hand, he would ominously tap me multiple times on the head while chanting some mantras by which he would attempt to cast out the spirits from my body. The ritual ended with a chug of his signature drink to drive out the spirits presumed to have possessed me.

Yearly festivals were held in jungle-like places where my extended family would gather and offer food offerings and animal blood in sacrifices to the deities. A tall, white tent was erected in the middle of the camp, where men clothed in white trousers could enter. Women were forbidden to enter the tent, but the men would take their sons inside to teach them about the ritual sacrifices that they would be expected to perform one day. I was up next.

I remember going into the tent as a child, no older than eight years of age. Upon entering the tent, I saw little stones forming a circle around the inside of the tent with food offerings and red powder sprinkled on them. Nearby stood a terrified goat tied to a pole, which was due to be sacrificed to the deities. I was then asked to recite the mantras and help one of the men conduct the sacrifice. My right hand was then placed over the man's right hand as he was holding a sharp knife and getting ready to slit the goat's throat.

Once an incision was performed, the goat was made to encircle the tent multiple times so that its blood could spray on the stones. When the goat was done bleeding out, it would then be beheaded. Furthermore, the decapitated head was then placed inside the tent as an offering to the deities. The carcass was taken outside, skinned, boiled, roasted, and feasted sumptuously upon by the festival attendees. Even the women were allowed to eat the sacrifice once the meat was prepared. This gruesome event was a sin-atoning ritual that took place every year. But this was only the beginning of my traumas.

It was at my uncle's house where I would witness something truly horrible. I was nine years old when I stumbled upon the footage of twelve Nepali workers who were captured and brutally killed by Islamic militants on a trip to Iraq. They were mistaken for American spies because of their English-speaking skills. By putting them to death publicly, the terrorists sought to communicate their disdain for America. The story made headlines all over the country in 2004.

Horror gripped me as I saw the terror-stricken faces of the captured Nepali men as they pleaded for mercy. They begged and begged to have their lives spared but to no avail. Eventually, eleven of them were shot dead, and the last man was beheaded. Sleep evaded me that night, not because of the horror I had witnessed on that screen but because of the questions that tormented my mind: Where did these men go after they passed? Will death come after me in the same unsuspecting way it did to them? It was then that I found myself desiring to live eternally.

After the 2004 incident, rioters swept the country of Nepal, destroying and burning everything in their way. Anger toward the Iraqis and the Nepali government, who had failed to ensure the safety of the twelve men, quickly led to more turmoil. Meanwhile, a civil war had broken out between the Maoists and those opposed to their communistic ideologies. Out in the streets, citizens of opposing political parties, united through raging anger, were destroying the very country that they were fighting to save. The latter were infuriated by years of government corruption and dishonesty. Although their feelings were well-warranted, their actions were counterproductive. By closing down educational systems, burning government properties, and rioting, they only made matters worse.

The political climate in Nepal has never been completely stable since the assassination of Nepal's most beloved king, Birendra, and his family in 2001. Shortly after the assassination, his brother assumed the throne. Maoists gained control of many villages and demanded that the new king step down. This resulted in the Maoist rebels attempting to forcefully remove the king and usurp the monarchy. Years of bloodshed and innumerable deaths followed as the Nepali Army and the Maoist insurgents warred against each other with no resolution in sight.

Finally, in 2006, the king stepped down and yielded executive authority to a new prime minister chosen by the political parties to oversee the return of democracy. During those years, no one was safe, especially the children of politically affiliated families and government officials. On many occasions, they were kidnapped by the Maoists and held for ransom. Body parts of dismembered children would then be found floating in rivers and dumped in trash heaps.

Unfortunately, my father worked as a government accountant. He was very much aware of the deteriorating situation within the country. There was civil unrest of such great proportion that those with families wanting peace started migrating to the United States, United Kingdom, Canada, and Australia. Despite my father always being an optimist, he knew then that the country he loved so dearly was no longer a place to raise his family. My father migrated to Australia in late 2007 to secure a new home for us. Six harrowing months later, my mother, sister, and I joined him.

So, with Nepal behind us and Australia before us, we made our descent to Sydney in March 2008. Once in Australia, while my father was studying and working full-time, my mother was getting acquainted with Australian culture and the English language. My sister and I were attending high school and excelling in understanding the Australian way of life. I soon started to pick up the Australian accent; and within a year, I spoke like a native.

As a twelve-year-old, I had no difficulty adapting to the culture. Seeing all the endless opportunities presented to me, the future looked promising.

Freedom meant choosing from all the endless possibilities and goals for the future. In vain, I tried to achieve inner freedom when, deep down, the thought of death still terrified and enslaved me. The fear of death had followed me to Australia and made its habitation in the inner chambers of my heart and soul. Chains of hopelessness bound me from within as I longed for deliverance from its power.

Plunging myself into reckless living seemed to be the only remedy for stopping the looming threat of death that plagued my mind. My reckless living included things like lying, cheating, stealing, drinking, drug abuse, and getting in trouble with the law. All this became a routine for me as a thirteen-year-old. Deep down, I knew that I committed these acts to drown out the constant reminder of death and the dreadful images of those I had lost to the pangs of it. The lawless flood of debauchery I welcomed into my life befriended the enemy I strove to flee from.

The idea of death became inescapable for me. For the first time in my life, I asked the question, "Why do we die?" Although my parents were apprehensive about me, they had no idea of the severity of the battle that waged within my soul. They began to blame one another for their decision to leave their country, believing their children would have been spared their turmoil had they stayed in Nepal. Things would get so bad that I even prayed to the household gods my mother had brought along from Nepal. The gods went wherever we went. They were packaged carefully and then displayed on a corner counter of our kitchen. It was to these gods that I prayed to in my heart, although I doubted that they would answer me. This went on for days; and then days became months, and months became years.

In early 2009, my father took a job offer in Adelaide, South Australia, where my life would only get worse. We quickly moved, and I continued the remainder of my high school years in Adelaide. By October 2011, I had hit rock bottom. Now sixteen years old and having exhausted every form of rebellion under the sun, I was sorely vexed in my soul. I soon found that there was no satisfaction in this immoral lifestyle. Surely, there was no reason to live and no hope of redemption to be found.

I recall drinking with my friends during this period, and we found ourselves conversing about vain earthly possessions, such as cars, nicer homes, beautiful women, and a six-figure income. Sadly, all my interest in these things had been lost. While the conversation went on, my heart was anguished. It cried out from within, "With all the money, degrees, possessions, and prominence, can my soul be ransomed from death?" Probably not.

That night, while I was being driven home, even while drunk, I felt the deepest, darkest, and most damning terror in my soul. Whispers of death penetrated my mind with questions like, "Do you know that I will come at an hour when you least expect Me? Where are those who labored all their lives for fame and fortune and are nowhere to be found or remembered because I called their name? Will your striving after all the earthly things deliver you from Me? Can you, with all your efforts combined, stop Me from snatching you at this very moment?"

Trembling at the last question, I went home and contemplated suicide. I could no longer continue to wrestle with these thoughts; they were killing me slowly. With that contemplation still fresh in my mind, sleep overtook me. Between 4:30 and 5:00 a.m., a Voice suddenly spoke and awakened me. In essence, the Voice was dreadful yet comforting. The words I was told were, "Get the Bible."

After hearing this, paralyzing fear gripped me. The comfort was knowing the certainty of the much-needed answers to the questions plaguing my soul. Sensing the urgency of this message and the bitter-awaited consequence if I neglected the words spoken by the Voice filled me with dread. I never doubted nor questioned the Voice that spoke to me; and without thinking, I submitted to the words spoken. My soul had finally felt a hint of peace that I had never experienced in my life.

Unable to fall asleep after that encounter, I found myself contemplating Who it was that had spoken to me. Growing up in Nepal, I was strictly cautioned never to fall into the snare of Christianity, since the Hindus perceived it as a money-making scheme called "the Church." I never questioned these claims any further or the reason behind the accusations of those called Christians. The Bible was never brought up in any conversation, let alone taught at home. Having overheard the immense cost of converting to Christianity on many occasions, I resolved never to bring shame and dishonor to my family. Altogether, this made the Christian religion undesirable for me.

After this incident, I found myself at a local bookshop that very morning and bought my first-ever New Testament Bible. Little did I know that my life would be turned upside down. The clerk at the bookshop pointed me toward the aisle where a copy could be found. My heart began to pound within my chest as I made my way to obtain the book. The memory of taking the Bible from the bookshelf, holding it firmly to my chest, closing my eyes, and gently whispering, "All should be well henceforth" was difficult to forget.

I could not wait to take this treasure home and read it. But as joyful as the moment was, the matter was to be kept secret from everyone, especially my family. I did not want to know what would happen if they ever found out that I had brought a Bible home. Even so, I spent the entire day reading the gospel accounts, beginning with Matthew. Every word in it spoke to my inner man, especially the Beatitudes spoken by Jesus, one of which was, "Blessed are the pure in heart, for they shall see God" (Matt. 5:8). With such verses came deep soul-searching questions, such as, "Where could this pure heart to have such an intimate relationship with God be obtained?"

Every word spoken by this man, Jesus of Nazareth, started to satisfy my soul's hungry, thirsty, and lonely depths. The following quote in particular made my greatest need unequivocally clear: "'Go and learn what this means: *I desire mercy, and not sacrifice. For I came not to call the righteous, but sinners*'" (Matt. 9:13). Reading such passages brought the memories of animal sacrifices flooding back. Nonetheless, each chapter I read elevated Jesus to an ever-exalted new height.

My heart longed to know more about this Man. His thirst-quenching teachings about sin, repentance, forgiveness, and salvation gripped my inner longings. I was expecting to read about Him becoming a mighty Ruler, Who would rid the world of all pain and suffering. But to my astonishment, reading of the betrayal, arrest, and death of Jesus left me instantly drowning in such great sorrow that it made my whole body tremble. They crucified Him!

I was so enraged and embittered that I threw the Bible against the wall. Then, bursting into tears, I cried out, "Why would those people kill such an innocent man? He never committed a crime but busied Himself with healing the sick, raising the dead, and casting out demons while preaching the kingdom of God. Why? Oh, why did they do it? Does death have the final say in a man's life? How could a perfect Man have been crucified and treated like the worst of criminals?" I had almost given up reading, if not for the Voice Who bid me, "Get the Bible," and then, "Continue reading."

It was not a Voice heard in the physical realm, but one my soul recognized and submitted to once again. With a slight glimmer of hope, I picked the scrunched-up Bible from the floor and continued reading the story of what followed after the crucifixion. All of a sudden, my emotions being stirred, I gasped at the reading of these Scriptures: "'He is not here, for he has risen, as he said. Come, see the place where he lay'" (Matt. 28:6) and "And behold, Jesus met them and said, 'Greetings!' And they came up and took hold of his feet and worshipped him" (Matt. 28:9).

All I could think was, "Could it be? Oh! Let it be so!" Tears started streaming down my cheeks as rejoicing and soul-soothing laughter overtook me, and I said to myself, "He lives, oh, He lives!" My first day of reading ended with the joy of knowing that the Man Jesus had conquered death. Lying in bed that night, holding the Bible to my chest, I slept as peacefully as a child. But soon, I would be overtaken by terror.

Sometime between 3:00 and 4:00 a.m., a dark, shadowy figure suddenly appeared beside me. There was no human explanation for what followed. I was conscious of my surroundings but unable to make out any faces due to being partly asleep. The figure sat on my bed beside me, and I felt the bed sink. From my peripheral, I was only able to make out its shape. It was that of a tall, giant man. The room was completely dark; and my body was paralyzed, making it impossible to identify the creature.

This was the devil, I thought to myself as I recalled reading about Satan, who tempted Jesus in the wilderness. The devil growled mockingly each time I struggled to break free from his awful presence. He started to strangle me until I could no longer fight him nor resist his power. I didn't know what I could do to free myself from the demonic grasp around my neck. Surely, I was done for. But then, something miraculous happened.

"I will surely die and not live," I said in such despair, when that all-familiar voice suddenly spoke to my soul, "Call upon the name of the Lord." I knew at that moment that this voice was none other than the Lord Jesus. I took courage and struggled with this shadowy figure to call the name of Jesus; and when finally I spoke—nay, I screamed from the top of my lungs—"In the name of Jesus of Nazareth! In the name of Jesus of Nazareth!" the fight ended.

Drenched in sweat, I awoke and found myself alone in that room, praising the Lord Jesus with a song of thanksgiving. My reading continued the next day from the Gospel according to Mark to the Book of Revelation. It felt as though my heart would burst from the weight of the glorious truths I was reading. With my heart now wide open to receive the truth, I felt the deepest and driest depths of my soul being nourished with the living waters of the Word of God. Not once do I recall doubting nor questioning God's Word.

Slowly, I began to understand the reason behind my existence—not what, but for Whom I was made—Jesus Christ. After reading the final book of the Bible, the soul-crushing weight of all the sins I had ever committed brought me to my knees. How could I approach this holy God with my sin-soaked soul? Passages from the Scriptures came flying back to me, such as, "'Come to me, all who labor and are heavy laden, and I will give you rest'" (Matt. 11:28). I fell asleep with these Scriptures in mind and treasured them in my heart.

My appetite was satiated by believing the words of Christ. There was no desire for earthly food, for I was filling my soul with heavenly riches. But these joy-filled moments would soon be replaced by a dreadful dream that occurred the same night. In the dream, I was cast down to what seemed like a bottomless pit. The deeper I went, the darker it got. This was no ordinary darkness; it was a darkness that could be felt. Screaming in exceeding fear, I realized that there was no coming back from that terrifying eternal destiny.

Thoughts and deeds of my poor, wasted, sinful life flashed before my eyes; and in agony, I cried for help. In desperation, I pleaded for mercy, wishing to be rescued from this indescribable place of terror. Then, to my relief, the resounding voice of the Lord pierced my heart and said, "Those 'who call upon the name of the Lord will be saved'" (Rom. 10:13). I screamed from the top of my lungs, "Lord Jesus, save me from this pit; save me, oh Lord!"

Suddenly, an outstretched arm, long enough to reach any length, pulled me out of that horrible pit. As I was being pulled up, I felt waves of comfort flood my soul; and just when praises were about to pour out of my lips, I awoke. By that time, it was around 5:00 a.m. I lay prostrate that early morning, confessing and forsaking all my sins, raised as a new creation in Christ Jesus, my Lord. With tear-mingled pleas for mercy, I said, "Lord, I want to live with You forever. I don't know how to pray, but I trust You can hear me. Forgive me, oh Lord, for all my unmentionable sins against You. Please, take me to be Yours, please."

I had been lost in an infinite loop of sin for so long, but now I was saved. The Lord Jesus had rescued me and showered my soul with mercy. His magnificent presence substituted the loneliness I had felt before. His compassion hemmed my sin-stained soul, and the heavy burden of sin that so gripped my inner man ceased to exist. Instead, the love of Christ was birthed in my heart, assuring me that I had been raised to a new, imperishable life. Three days of reading, groaning, and weeping over my wretched condition resulted in glorious salvation. From the deadness of my former life and the domain of darkness, I was transferred into His glorious light. Just as the Lord Jesus rose from the dead on the third day, I, too, rose to a new life, which similarly occurred on the third day after completing my study of the New Testament.

CHAPTER 2

OUT OF MY SIN AND INTO THYSELF

"Since you have been born again, not of perishable seed but of imperishable, through the living and abiding word of God."

1 Peter 1:23

THESE BEAUTIFUL, DIVINELY INSPIRED WORDS were penned down by Peter, one of Jesus Christ's beloved disciples. With this knowledge, I was ready to serve the Lord, Who had made me His own. No longer would I be a slave to the corruption of sin that had held me captive. Serving the Lord with the remainder of my fleeting days became the supreme desire of my heart.

All of this philosophizing took place within the inner workings of my room, the walls of which were once a prison cell but now a place of freedom. I had walked into that room as a hopeless teenager contemplating suicide; and thanks to His grace, I walked out a new creature. However, as joy-filled as I was, my mother was very concerned because of the sounds of groans and bitter weeping coming out of my room.

My mother often knocked to check up on me, but I assured her everything was fine. Actually, "fine" was an understatement. Everything was supernaturally wonderful! Leaving the room for the first time in three days, I slipped into the backyard; and with a new set of eyes, I beheld the creation of God: the skies, the trees, the flowers, the butterflies, and the birds flying and singing in unison, reflecting the glory and craftsmanship of the Lord. With the little breath left in me, I closed my eyes, bowed my knees, and cried out, "Now I live!"

Adoring the Lord with shouts of praise in worship, I burst forth in thanksgiving for the mercy that I had now received and for which I was forever indebted. In my newfound joy, I went to my mother and shared how I had been saved.

She replied, "Saved from what?"

"From myself, my sins, and all idolatry," I replied.

"And what saved you from these?" she asked.

"Not what but rather Who—and His name is Jesus Christ! He saved me; He saved me! He is God," I replied.

"Sure," she said. "He is no different from the gods we serve."

"No, Mother; He is not a god. He is the only true and living God. There is no one else like Him or beside Him."

Furious at the response, she shouted, "Enough! No more of this. Would you dare blaspheme the gods that have been our guides for centuries?"

"Mum," I replied, "these are idols, the work of man's hand. How can we bow and worship before a man-made image? I have prayed to them in my distress; and in vain did I utter my petitions to them, for they never answered. But when I prayed to the God of the Bible, unlike the gods we serve, He came to my rescue and saved my soul from the death sentence I had received from serving sin and the devil all these years. We must burn and cast these idols away and together turn to the only One Who can bring salvation to our needy souls."

"That is enough!" she shouted. "No more of this! I was born into the Hindu religion and will gladly die in it. Shake it off! You are in Australia, but you will always be Nepali until death. Hinduism is the oldest and truest religion. You will always be a Hindu."

Filled with newborn zeal for the Lord, I responded, "Mother, you are following this religion because it was taught to you by your parents. Concerning the blessed Lord Jesus' revelation to me, I did not find Him nor search for Him. He found me and revealed Himself to me. I know the truth. He is the Truth. I am not turning back."

I could see my mother's face turning redder by the second. Infuriated with my response, she ran into my room and found the Bible. She lifted it and inquired, "This is what you believe in?" In a fury, she threw the Bible across the room and stormed out as I calmly reassured her of my love. This drama was only the beginning of my family woes that came with my new conversion.

News of my conversion soon spread to my father and then to our extended families in Nepal. It felt like a wedge had been placed between my family and me. With this new reality check, I began praying unceasingly for my family's salvation. On the other hand, my dear sister never expressed much emotion. She was a deep thinker and always kept matters to herself. Therefore, the news of my conversion did not trouble her as much as it did my parents. Tensions soon built up in the home as I no longer participated in Hindu festivals or celebrations.

I longed for a Christian friend, but the sorrow of seeing my loved ones on the verge of destruction kept me locked up in my room for days and nights in the Word of God and prayer. Weeping for my family left me with no more tears to offer to the Lord. At times, my mother would get so angry and renounce me in the heat of the moment and strongly urge me to leave the house. I knew this couldn't be allowed to continue much longer.

For three long years, I was left to myself without a brother or a sister. Had it not been for the Word of God encouraging me in those lonely and troublesome times, sorrow would have swallowed me up. Because of this constant risk, prayer was as essential to me as air to my lungs. In addition, my understanding of the Church and discipleship was not yet fully developed. Thus, I could feel the level of spiritual hunger that I once possessed quickly drowned out by isolation.

"Lord!" I cried out one night, "Who have I here except You? Will You direct my path and lead me to where I need to be?"

It was now the year 2014 when I felt a constant, nagging desire to migrate to the United States. I gave myself over to prayer in response to this feeling, and the Lord opened a door for me to journey across the Pacific Ocean. In September 2014, I packed my belongings, left Australia, hit the skies, and headed toward Colorado, USA. Every step of the way, I put my trust in the Lord and cast my fears and burdens on Him for all that lay ahead.

Upon arriving in Colorado, I breathed a sigh of relief and whispered, "Lord, I am here. Lead me onward."

As refreshed as I was on my new journey in America, something still nagged at my inner being. My heart longed to befriend a fellow Christian brother. Through hearsay, I had heard that the United States was a Christian nation with churches everywhere. This rumor led me to search for an American Christian who would get me acquainted with a body of believers—the Church.

In the meanwhile, the following words of my Lord Jesus filled the void: "When he saw the crowds, he had compassion for them, because they were harassed and helpless, like sheep without a shepherd. Then he said to his disciples, 'The harvest is plentiful, but the laborers are few; therefore pray earnestly to the Lord of the harvest to send out laborers into his harvest'" (Matt: 9:36-38).

The Lord was beginning to kindle my heart with fiery zeal for evangelism and, at the same time, open my eyes to see the masses in the light of eternity. Before I knew it, my long-awaited and prayerful desire to meet Christians had been granted through Divine Providence. Under unusual circumstances, I met new brothers in Christ one after another. One brother in particular, who was an evangelist, played an influential role in my early Christian walk. He asked me to accompany him to one of his street evangelism meetings.

"Why not?" I replied. Surely, I would love to watch and learn. Or so I thought. There were no words to describe the intense urgency of this man's words as he implored the bystanders to repent and put their trust in Jesus Christ. I felt as though I were listening to John the Baptist preach fearlessly against a Herod-like crowd. Surprisingly, the people who opposed the message in the streets were not nearly as bad as those who professed faith in the Lord Jesus Christ but whose actions dictated otherwise.

What I meant by this was, for example, that the word "repent" seemed to anger many lukewarm churchgoers as they felt judged by the message of true Christianity. Anyway, as these conflicting worlds collided in my head, out of nowhere I was given the bullhorn and asked to start preaching. At the request alone, my hands and feet began trembling at the thought of preaching out loud to angry strangers. Miraculously, though, with faith the size of a mustard seed, I whispered a prayer to the Lord. "Oh, Lord, You must speak through me."

What started as a soft-spoken voice quickly changed its tone to what I can only describe as the sound of a trumpet cry. The Spirit of God clothed me with such power to preach on repentance and true conversion that an entire hour had passed by, and I perceived it not. Unfortunately, my message of Christ was received with great mockery and scorn. Feeling rejected by men but securing the Lords's smile, my new friend and I left rejoicing, knowing the Lord had implanted seeds in the most rebellious of hearts. From that moment on, evangelism became a joyous task; and we found ourselves preaching the gospel every day to every creature.

It was now clear that God had called me to be an evangelist. With plenty of time to spare due to not working in the United States because of visa restrictions, I gave myself over to prayer, studying the Word of God, and street evangelism. During those days, I lost track of time simply because the Spirit of God had descended upon my heart. Hungry for deeper revelations from the Word of God, He lifted my soul to great heights of understanding and great depths of meditations. I beheld the sufficiency of Christ's sacrifice with new adorning eyes and His blood to save and cleanse people from all sin with revived gratitude. Thus, spending up to nine hours a day studying the Scriptures and searching diligently for anything about Christ filled my periods of joy-filled isolation.

Outside of my hours of studying, back in the streets of Colorado, a common reoccurrence was often encountering Christians who opposed the message of holy living. Even a preacher from a local church I often attended was greatly annoyed when I encouraged a teenager to a life of holiness and fear of the Lord. I did this by referring to a passage of Scripture: "Strive for peace with everyone, and for the holiness without which no one will see the Lord" (Heb. 12:14). His annoyance at my encouragement to the youth drove him to state that "holiness is relationally granted to believers when they become Christians; therefore, Christians need not focus on pursuing it."

To make his point, the preacher painted a picture of a son inheriting his father's last name because of his relationship with the father. This meant the same for a believer in Jesus Christ and the holiness He granted because of a believer's relationship with Him. This statement, although true in some parts, lacked support from the Scriptures themselves. It was mostly just a feel-good jargon. Tragically, this would become a trend across Colorado as I met more lukewarm Christians.

As the day came to an end and night fell, I was led to meditate upon a Scripture:

> For the grace of God has appeared, bringing salvation for all people, training us to renounce ungodliness and worldly passions, and to live self-controlled, upright, and godly lives in the present age, waiting for our blessed hope, the appearing of the glory of our great God and Savior Jesus Christ, who gave himself for us to redeem us from all lawlessness and to purify for himself a people for his own possession who are zealous for good works (Titus 2:11-14).

In addition, the following verses also echoed in my mind: "As obedient children, do not be conformed to the passions of your former ignorance, but as he who called you is holy, you also be holy in all your conduct, since it is written, 'You shall be holy, for I am holy'" (1 Pet. 1:14-16). Upon meditating on these words, I realized that the grace of God actively trained a believer to renounce ungodliness and pursue a godly living. The Scriptures were clear that holiness was not merely a matter of one's creed and belief in one's identity as a child of God; but rather, it was to be displayed and proven through conduct that flows from the character of those who have been born again.

"So why would a believer not pursue holiness if they have been given the grace to do so?" I asked myself. After some deep thought, I answered myself, "The same grace that brought people to salvation was also the same grace that empowered a believer to keep their life pure, both internally and externally. It was God Who purified believers and made them zealous for good works after having cleansed them from all sin."

As time went on, my knowledge of spiritual matters grew. With that in mind, from the years 2015-2016, the Lord enabled me to travel throughout the USA to evangelize. They were years of exponential growth in grace and sanctification. I desired "power from on high" to evangelize, which then led me into night-long intercessions and fasting, where my soul began to treasure the words of His mouth more than my portions of earthly food. Unbeknownst to me, God was already paving my path for the future. Toward the end of 2015, I met a beautiful young lady at a youth meeting near the church where I lived. Her brother, whom I had met before, introduced us.

After discovering her family's missionary ventures and upbringing in Brazil among the Amazonians, I wanted to meet her again for coffee and talk further on this matter. Miss Julie took up the invitation, and we met again for coffee. After hearing of the wonderful work of grace in the Amazon throughout the years of her parents' work as missionaries to the tribes, I wanted to know more. So she told me everything. For example, she told me about what was originally only a vision of her parents to start an orphanage, which then became a reality. Before her parents knew it, hundreds of orphans would come under the loving protection of the Lord Jesus Christ, as it came to fruition in the first decade of the twenty-first century. But as wonderful as all this was to learn, I had a more important question to ask.

Holding nothing back, I directed a specific question toward her. As our meeting was ending, I asked her, "What about yourself? How were you saved?"

She replied, "What do you mean? I have always been a Christian."

"Have you been born again?" I asked.

There was a long pause; and after a minute or so had passed, I asked, "Do you know Him?"

Tears of confession and repentance started streaming down her cheeks as she cried out, "I've known about Him all my life, but Him I do not know."

The Lord birthed such great anguish as He opened her eyes to behold His perfect holiness and her exceeding sinfulness. As with me several years ago, Miss Julie was a new creation in Christ Jesus on this night. Time went on; and within sixteen months of growing in the grace and love of the Lord Jesus Christ, we were married the following April and ready to serve the Lord as one. Since April 2017, we have served the Body of Christ in various places in the United States. Now, we are raising six wonderful children in the fear of the Lord and the comfort of His Spirit.

I received many wonderful gifts from my Father in Heaven. Among these gifts were a good family, wonderful friends, and a marvelous new place to call home in Colorado. However, one gift that surpassed them all has been the revelation of the riches of His Word. As underserving as I am of all His graces and wisdom that He has so freely bestowed, it is only fitting that I should likewise speak to you freely of Christ's love and passion for His Church and the lost world at large. . Therefore, let us, oh brethren, draw from the deepest wells of His salvation to discover the thirst-quenching, hunger-ceasing, soul-soothing, and heart-rending truth of the cross and the obedience it demands!

CHAPTER 3

DO YOU KNOW HIM?

"Whoever says 'I know him' but does not keep his commandments is a liar, and the truth is not in him."

1 John 2:4

THERE ARE MILLIONS OF PEOPLE who profess the name of the Lord Jesus Christ who attend church services, conferences, youth meetings, and all sorts of seminaries. This all sounds marvelous because it indicates that people should be absolutely on fire for the Lord and live a life of holiness. Yet people are sinking into severe moral and spiritual decline at an exponential rate.

I state this about those supposed believers in our Lord Jesus Christ. Many of us are utterly unconcerned about the Word of God and prayer, let alone evangelism. No wonder darkness fills the land, and the people are grossly wicked. While adding one thing to another, I realized that it is not our lack of Bible reading and prayer that has rendered the Church's work in the world powerless and ineffective but, instead, regeneration.

How many of those who say they believe *actually* believe? We would do well not to point fingers when the problem lies within. In addition, what is going on and why is not a big mystery. The answer is found in John 3:3: "'Truly, truly, I say to you, unless one is born again he cannot see the kingdom of God.'" Furthermore, Jesus goes on to say in John 3:7, "Do not marvel that I said to you, *You must be born again.*'" I would dare say that eighty out of a hundred people I have evangelized to throughout the years were churchgoers who had never heard the term "born again," let alone its implications. That is a terrifying reality, where potentially, millions of people are dead in their sins and bound for Hell, all the while believing that they are actually Heaven-bound.

During my early years of street evangelism, I often asked the question, "Are you a Christian?"

Most would reply, "Well, I go to church, or I was raised in the church."

As unsettling as these answers were, I never questioned anybody further regarding the fruit of their conversion, which was a private matter among many churchgoers.

Could it be that we have millions who are headed to damnation, all the while professing the name of the Lord yet bearing no fruit worthy of repentance? Unfortunately, the answer is yes. On any given Sunday, the pews are filled with the damned, heading to Hell with indifference on their faces. This tragic genocide is occurring because they were never told that they must be born again to enter the kingdom of Heaven.

So what does it mean to be born again? The phrase *born again* or *born from above* simply means that God comes to make His habitation in you the moment you believe in the gospel of Jesus Christ. The blessed Spirit of God inhabits you and births in you a new heart and desires which are now acceptable and pleasing to God. Thus, the saying from 2 Corinthians 5:17 comes to pass: "If anyone is in Christ, he is a new creation. The old has passed away; behold, the new has come." The old man in Adam passes away, and the new man in Christ Jesus is born. According to the Word of God, having been born from above, this new man desires the things from above.

That being said, as a new creation, a new believer is basically a baby in theological knowledge. This newly born infant in Christ Jesus will then need to grow in their love for the Lord and the brethren for whom Christ died, along with many other beautiful graces such as delighting in the Word of God, prayer, and evangelism. Understandably, this is a lot for someone to take in as a new believer. Slowly but surely, though, the new creature will desire more and more the fruit of a spirit-filled life. But how exactly is someone born again as a new creation?

To be born again, you must repent. At the start of His ministry, our Lord Jesus preached on repentance and faith, as we read in the following account, "Now after John was arrested, Jesus came into Galilee, proclaiming the gospel of God, and saying, 'The time is fulfilled, and the kingdom of God is at hand; repent and believe the gospel'" (Mark 1:14-15). Repentance is a recurring theme throughout the Bible, especially in the New Testament, yet it has become an intolerable word among many church-goers. True repentance is changing one's mind to focus on God's things through accepting His truth. It is to sorrowfully renounce the sinner's wicked condition as the eyes of one's heart behold God—the One against Whom they have sinned. The sorrow we speak of here is a godly one that produces repentance (2 Cor. 7:10), which casts the sinner out of his sin and into God's mercy. It is turning away from all evil and turning to God.

True repentance is a two-fold act that includes turning away from something and turning toward something new. The former is powerless if not followed up by the latter. You must turn from your sins; but if you only stop there, it will not deliver you from falling back into it. Therefore, you must turn to God from your sins because "our God is a God of salvation, and to God, the Lord, belong deliverances from death" (Psalm 68:20). One of the many signs of a maturing Christian is their continuing growth in repentance and faith resulting from their salvation.

In contrast, the false convert claims salvation with no evidence of change in either of these areas. The faith I read about in the Word of God only resulted in true salvation. But alas, many people who claim to believe in the gospel of salvation are stuck in a lukewarm pool of stagnation. True repentance is granted with faith. Faith then secures forgiveness, which results in cleansing; and cleansing begets purity, and purity beholds His presence.

However, something that should be one of our biggest strengths is actually where many believers are weak.

Here lies our weakness: evangelism. This weakness or even total lack of evangelism can be attributed to our prayerlessness, which is a good indicator of our direct relationship with God. After having evangelized to scores of people in the United States, one thing is crystal clear: many do not know God! They know about Him vaguely because of their Sunday attendance; but alas, Monday through Saturday becomes a time of self-worship, as many go about their businesses. The week becomes a period where God is forgotten and the needs of the self take priority.

Listen, when you become Christian, you are no longer your own. You're dead and dying daily to yourself. Jesus Christ owns you. He spilled His blood to redeem you from all lawlessness, and it doesn't end there. According to the Word of God, you are now called to a life of holiness (2 Tim. 1:9) and saved for good works (Eph. 2:10). With that in mind, out of the seven churches mentioned in the Bible's Book of Revelation, five are known to the Lord by their works. So while works do not bring salvation, they are, in fact, a strong indicator of whether someone is saved at all. Furthermore, our Lord Jesus Himself states that those who do the Father's will shall enter the kingdom of God (Matt. 7:21). Therefore, as a result of saving faith, the true believer devotes himself to the service of his Lord.

CHAPTER 4

EVANGELISM

"For we cannot but speak of what we have seen and heard."

Acts 4:20

IN THIS MORALLY DECLINING DAY and age, we desperately need Spirit-filled apostolic preaching, the likes of which we've only read about in the Book of Acts. We have busied ourselves with too much planning, strategizing, networking, and conferencing about the latest trends in evangelism when the surest way is found in a person and not human methods. This person is the blessed Spirit of God Himself, Who inhabits us with the power to witness (Acts 1:8). Evangelism is not a natural task but a spiritual one. These radical yet straightforward ideas can all be found in the Bible.

The Bible is full of things that make little sense to an overly rational mind. For example, if you read Acts 2:22-41, you will find the apostle Peter's preaching to a crowd at Pentecost. He starts by talking about Christ's humiliation, resurrection, and exaltation there. After these soul-piercing words, Peter urged the crowd to look within themselves because they were the ones who had put Christ to death. Peter's bold preaching resulted in three thousand souls being saved and baptized from the vast crowd that listened to his message. An incredible miracle resulted from a simple, spirit-filled fisherman speaking his heart out. No significant education was required, just faith and a life of complete obedience.

Many people these days attribute their works of folly to the blessed Spirit's influence. Here is a sure sign of the Spirit's work: "He will glorify me, for he will take what is mine and declare it to you'" (John 16:14). Jesus Christ must be glorified in you before He can be glorified through you. For this to happen, one must strive to become a pure vessel. A pure vessel is who the Lord delights using (2 Tim. 2:20-21). But how does one develop the desire to be pure?

Intimacy in prayer and deep studying of the Scriptures will cause you to joyfully submit to His will. I remember preaching about the mercy and love of God at a street meeting, where there was a substantial gathering. All was well until sin, repentance, and Hell became the central theme in the preaching. Then, people in the crowd that had gathered started to leave one by one. Some people sneered at the preaching and left the scene with mockery and shouting cuss words. These types of reactions happened quite often, which beget in me a hunger to search out the Scriptures to confirm the message I was preaching for myself, lest I had run in vain.

Later that night, the Spirit led me to read John 6, where many of His disciples turned back and no longer walked with Jesus due to His preaching. They were thinking about their earthly flesh while the Lord talked to them about the Spirit Who gave life (John 6:63). Indeed, "the peace of God, which surpasses all understanding" (Phil. 4:7) was given to me that night, as I was shown the fear and love which I had for the Word of the Lord and how it would preserve me from snares and pitfalls (Psalm 119:165). From that moment on, I desired Christ's approval at the expense of man's rejection. Likewise, we should all be the most satisfied when God is always glorified.

Let us return to Spirit-birthed evangelism through Spirit-filled men. We are given the ministry of reconciliation and entrusted with the message of God to reunite the world through Christ, not counting their trespasses against them (2 Cor. 5:18-19). The apostle Paul presents this glorious truth with great emotion as he cries out these words through the Holy Spirit, "We implore you on behalf of Christ, be reconciled to God" (2 Cor. 5:20). In this self-centered age, the most dominating evangelistic message I have heard preached to a

Christless multitude went something like this: "God loves you." While this is part of the gospel, it does not include the complete picture.

We cannot emphasize or favor one attribute of God at the expense of others. God is God for all that He is. It is His gospel, and it should be preached according to His ways. Furthermore, when reading the account of the early church in the Book of Acts, we do not find the word "love" mentioned in any of the apostles' preaching or anywhere else in the book. What we do see is a strong emphasis on one man, Jesus Christ. The early Church's preaching, persecution, poverty, and perseverance resulted from their faith in this Man, Whom they preached as the crucified, resurrected, and holy Judge. Moreover, through faith in Him, people could receive forgiveness of sins (Acts 10:39-43).

I believe the true love of God is that which we behold in the acts of Christ as we unpack the cross through proclaiming the gospel in its entirety. This is because the power to save lives is in the gospel of Jesus Christ, as it is written in Romans 1:16. Therefore, let us not magnify the comforts of His love without first presenting in length the cross that won it for us. Although God's love is glorious and beautiful, it is not the whole story of Who He is and how He made a way for sinful humanity to be saved and reunified with Him. But sadly, incomplete gospel messages remain popular in the pulpit and pews.

For example, an elderly church-goer once stated that she hadn't heard the preacher speak on the topic of Hell in many years. Thus, she deemed the preaching of sin and repentance archaic and counterproductive in winning souls to God and offensive, even for Christians. Instead, she suggested that love be the theme of evangelism by which souls are to be won to Christ. And yet, is it not the love of God through the display of His kindness that leads men to repentance, as it says in Romans 2:4 and 2 Peter 3:15? Was it not the Lord, in His great love, calling the lukewarm professors in Laodicea to repent as mentioned in Revelation 3:19? Did the early church not rejoice after hearing that Gentiles were granted repentance that led to eternal life (Acts 11:18)? Should we not proclaim repentance for the forgiveness of sins when it is a direct command from the Lord Himself (Luke 24:47)? Of course, we should.

In their call for salvation, repentance was the primary emphasis in the apostles' preachings among the Jews and Gentiles, as mentioned in Acts 2:38, 3:19-20, 17:30-21, 20:21, and 26:20. The cursed preaching of all-love and no-repentance movement is a common trend in churches that shows no signs of going out of style soon.

Finally, did our Lord Himself not emphasize that without repentance, all will perish (Luke 13:1-5)? So, in this case, we must obey the Word of God over the words of men—and even the words of our own preacher. The love of God is vigorously preached from many pulpits today, but I do not believe it is the same love of God that comes from the heart of the Holy Spirit. For if it were, our evangelism would be filled with intense longing and pleading for the billions groping in the dark. When was the last time you were up all night in anguished intercession for those at the brink of death and headed to the slaughter (Prov. 24:11-12)?

The Great Commission came with a call to preach the gospel and make disciples. We must remind ourselves that the Word of God is alive and active (Heb. 4:12); and when preached, it should produce a salt-like effect in an open wound that burns the unbelieving heart with the conviction of sin. Where there is no conviction of sin, there is no true gospel preaching. This conviction is what makes a person's soul search for the answers to one of the most profound matters possible—salvation.

And remember, this conviction can lead to either an increasing hardness that further separates someone from God or brokenness of the heart that makes someone run to the cross. Because of the seriousness of handling people's souls in preaching, we had better represent the Lord in all His fullness as it is required of ambassadors (2 Cor. 5:20). In his address to the Ephesian elders, the apostle Paul states, "Therefore I testify to you this day that I am innocent of the blood of all, for I did not shrink from declaring to you the whole counsel of God" (Acts 20:26-27). Either we proclaim God in all His fullness, or it is time we reconsider our calling as a preacher. The moment we shrink from declaring the entirety of the Word is when we incur the blood of those from whom we hid the truth. Let us be warned in the words of our Lord Jesus, "'For whoever is ashamed of me and my words, of him will the Son of Man be ashamed when he comes in his glory and the glory of the Father and of the holy angels'" (Luke 9:26).

With fierce loyalty to God, unceasing love for His Word, and a war-making approach to sin, you will welcome misunderstandings and even persecution from within the Church. Persecution is typically thought of as something done by outside forces; but for the most part, persecution comes from within the church walls. While not physically deadly, it can have a discouraging effect on a believer's heart.

Let's consider Christ's experience. The Pharisees did not persecute the Lord Jesus for His faith in the God of Israel but, rather, because of His pure obedience to Him. Likewise, those who take the Lord at His word hold it fast in an honest and good heart and bear fruit with patience (Luke 8:15). The company of those who have unwavering obedience, passion, and devotion endure criticisms from the Church and are described as fanatics by those who claim the mantle of Christianity due to relational and cultural ties.

CHAPTER 5
CALLED TO HOLINESS

"Since we have these promises, beloved, let us cleanse ourselves from every
defilement of body and spirit, bringing holiness to completion in the fear of God."

2 Corinthians 7:1

THE WORD ONCE TREASURED BY the early church has now become the dread of the modern church. Holiness reveals unholiness just as light reveals darkness. God's holiness exposes man's sinfulness. Likewise, a believer walking in the light of holiness reveals those walking in the darkness of unholiness. In return, unholiness retaliates with hatred and does not come to the light, lest its works be exposed (John 3:20). Holiness often gets equated with perfection and self-righteousness; for most, this is reason enough never to pursue it. After all, what makes us tremble more than having to hear the call to perfection?

To many, holiness has become nothing more than a head-filled doctrinal statement rather than a heart-filled pursuit. It is righteousness obtained by faith in Jesus Christ that makes a believer's pursuit of holiness or sanctification possible. Righteousness is by faith alone, while holiness or sanctification is the ongoing fruit of that obtained righteousness and its end—eternal life (Rom. 6:22). We are called saints as those who have been "set apart as holy, useful to the master of the house, ready for every good work" (2 Tim. 2:21). Holiness in salvation grants us our identity as saints, whereas holiness of salvation is the renewing work of grace by the power of the Spirit within, displayed without.

Now, let us talk about practical holiness, which happens to be one of the most heated topics in many churches and gets quickly shunned and labeled as legalism. There are many buzz words preached from our pulpits today, one of which happens to be legalism. In short, legalism is salvation by works. Many have gravely misused it to talk themselves out of obedience to the Lord. Holiness for salvation can be rightly termed as legalism, but holiness through salvation is unmistakably a biblical call; for without it, no one will see the Lord (Heb. 12:14).

Let us not mistake obedience for legalism. Our Lord puts it this way: "'If anyone would come after me, let him deny himself and take up his cross daily and follow me'" (Luke 9:23). For Christ to live in a man, the man must be crucified to himself (Gal. 2:20). He died for us that we might live for Him (2 Cor. 5:15). We show our utmost gratitude and love for His sacrifice through obedience (John 14:15). The holiness of the believer shines through obedience, and God's holy work of salvation makes a man holy both in character and conduct (1 Peter 1:15-16).

Do we not rightly call Him the Holy Spirit? He is holy and will not inhabit an unholy man who remains yet dead in trespasses and sins. Those whom the Son sets free are free indeed (John 8:36); likewise, those whom the Spirit indwells are made holy and continue therein. That is primarily what distinguishes a Spirit-filled man from a carnal man. The Holy Spirit will never honor a vessel that dishonors the Son, let alone grant His precious gifts to such a kind. He comes to live in those who embrace the work of the cross by offering themselves to a life of obedience (Acts 5:32).

So if the blessed Spirit is in you, why should you not desire and pursue after holiness? After all, He is our Helper; and the desire for holiness will bring Him speedily to your aid. You should rightly examine yourself to see whether you are in the faith should you be devoid of these graces (2 Cor. 13:5).

But to grow in holiness, we must thrive in the knowledge of the Holy One. This is done by abiding in the words of our Lord Jesus Christ (John 17:17). We are His disciples if we abide in His words. You can quote Scriptures by the hundreds, boast about revelations, go into details about dreams and visions, and never be a threat to the devil. He is well-versed and educated in the Word of God. It is not quoting God's Word that gets the devil to tremble as much as being habited by the One Who inspires the Word.

Holy men filled with the Holy Spirit are dreaded in Hell. Not only did God know the apostle Paul by name, but also, so did demons. In an attempted exorcism, seven men from a religious family were invoking the name of Jesus Christ, to which the demon replied, "'Jesus I know, and Paul I recognize, but who are you?'" Those men fled that house naked and wounded after the demon overpowered them (Acts 19:13-16). Even demons can discern between holy possessors of faith from unholy professions of it.

Believers' holiness is the ongoing work of the Spirit of God in the new man, which is being renewed in knowledge after the image of its creator (Col. 3:10). We desire holiness because we have been made holy. The works of our faith are discussed to greater lengths by the apostle Paul as he strongly exhorts believers to a lifestyle of holiness (Eph. 4:17-32, 5:3-6; Col. 3:5-10). One of God's definitive wills for the believer is holiness in the form of sexual purity. While sin itself is the separating factor between God and His creatures, some sins carry in themselves greater effects and consequences, one of which is sexual immorality (1 Cor. 6:13-20). "Flee!" is the cry of escape from the apostle Paul regarding this specific sin (2 Tim. 2:22). If only these so-called preachers trumpeted that command, we would have spared many souls from moral, spiritual, and mental desolation.

Woe to the preachers who have made peace with their congregants' sinfulness while disregarding and grieving God's holiness and, remind you, all in the name of love. Whoever says I love God and yet continues to walk in darkness disregards the God they profess to love (1 Thess. 4:3-8; 1 John 3:6;

1 John 2:4-6). After all, the love of God will never rejoice at wrongdoing but will always rejoice with the truth (1 Cor. 13:6).

How long shall we honor man's happiness at the cost of dishonoring God's holiness? God's holiness is honored, even in the face of adversity, when man's joy becomes all the more sweetly satisfying. If God is the Source of our exceeding joy, then His good pleasure should be our highest aim. The grace-filled yet graceless preaching of our day is drawing scores of curious inquirers who desire Heaven without a holy God. They want the crown of Christianity without its cross, its gold without its digging, and its mantle without its sackcloth. They also desire its power without holiness, its satisfaction without submission, and its piety without prayer. Therefore, they are being accommodated to receive a god that is palatable. Grace, which trains the believer to renounce ungodliness, is sadly being used as a license for sinfulness. This is due to preachers presenting forgiveness without repentance, grace without truth, comfort without the cross, and love without obedience.

By so doing, we are producing fruitless trees and branches ready to be cut down and thrown into the fire (Luke 3:9; John 15:6). The message of our Lord Jesus to the woman caught in adultery—"'Neither do I condemn you; go, and from now on sin no more'" (John 8:11)—was given after she acknowledged His supreme Authority as Lord. Notice the command was not to sin less but rather to sin no more. We live as though the former was the case. For condemnation to be removed, the heart must yield to the Lord to Whom belongs forgiveness. Condemnation was always there due to our being dead in trespasses and sins, but He came to save us from the condemnation that sin brought (John 3:18). Therefore, it is those who walk not according to the flesh but the Spirit who are delivered from the punishment of sin (Rom. 8:1-4).

If the result of His holiness in the Heavenly atmosphere causes the hosts to worship night and day before the throne (Rev. 4:6-11, 7:11-12, 11:16), how much more should the former enemies, now turned friends, bow their hearts in adoration to Him, of whose holiness they've tasted? You only have to fear holiness if you remain unyielded to the Lord and continue to present your members to sin as instruments for unrighteousness. But if you love the Lord with all your ransomed being, you will find yourself befriending holiness and abhorring sinfulness. The nearer you are to the Lord, the further you will be from sin.

Sin separates the unbeliever from God (Isa. 59:2), whereas holiness separates the believer from sin. Holiness is unattractive to a man whose portion is with the world, but it is a pursuit of utmost delight to them whose portion is above (1 John 3:1-3). The believer's holiness is persistent in its pursuit for purity of heart. It is jealous for God's glory and is fueled with desires to make much of it. But this type of holiness will cost you your family (Matt. 10:34-36), friends (1 Peter 4:3-5), and even your life (Matt. 14:1-12). The believer's power points to his personal holiness, which is the result of his yielded life; and that life is drawn through his pure devotion to the Holy One in prayer.

CHAPTER 6

PRAYERLESS PANDEMIC

"The prayer of a righteous person has great power as it is working."

James 5:16

WHILE I WAS GROWING UP, one thing was constantly pressing upon my heart: the passion and devotion with which the temple priests worshipped their deities. Some were so devoted that they sold possessions, denied themselves certain foods and drinks, shunned pleasure, and spent their fleeting days at the temple serving their gods. I never made eye contact with the deities during our visits to the temple, so I always turned my attention to the priests who would help the worshippers with their offerings and sacrifices. Tears would stream down their cheeks as they recited mantras and offered incense with prayers as an appeal to the deities for a swift response. Although I never desired the priestly garment, I found myself strangely drawn to their unwavering commitment and continuous desire for worship. They disciplined their bodies by chanting priestly mantras, which were strictly observed and kept by those desiring freedom from sin. Commitment to purity drove some to many extremes. These extreme actions included sleepless days and nights filled with meditation and starvation in hopes of one day attaining perfect holiness.

Oh, Christian, ask yourself, should a self-denying heathen priest, who sacrifices his life in worship, have more to present before demons than you do before the living God, Who redeemed you with His own blood? Can a

Christian bought by the blood of Christ be surpassed in devotion by those serving blood-thirsty devils? No, perish the thought. The lack of passion in the Christian's devotion is due to their prayerless state. Every act of disobedience can be tied to one's disregard for their prayer closet. Many men would have been spared from deception and pitfalls if they had sought the Lord's counsel in the first place. Consider Joshua's covenant with the Gibeonites (Josh. 9:14-15), a decision made without prayer that led the nation toward idolatry in the years to come (Num. 33:55; Judges 2:3-4). To his own peril, Saul chose the counsel of a medium over the Lord's (1 Chron. 10:13-14). King Rehoboam's evil decisions and actions were due to not seeking the Lord (2 Chron. 12:14). As the fowler rejoices over its senseless prey caught in the snare, so does the devil rejoice over a prayerless Christian caught in deception. Who will stand with Heaven and decry the prayerlessness of our churches?

A life devoid of prayer lacks genuine and enduring devotion to God. God has no shortcuts for the spiritually lazy person to reach a close relationship with Him. You must "draw near to God" for God to "draw near to you" (James 4:8). We have been granted all things pertaining to life and godliness (2 Peter 1:3); therefore, we have neither the devil nor any man to blame for not laying hold of what is at our disposal. There is only one person that keeps you from praying—yourself.

The entertainment-seeking Christian is bent on choosing relaxation over prostration, self-care over selfless prayer, possession over passion, exaltation over humiliation, and more of the television screen over God's presence unseen. Oh, slumbering Christian, put off the garments of prayerlessness and clothe yourself with affliction, mourning, and weeping! Let your laughter be turned to mourning and your joy to heaviness. Your prayerless condition testifies against your idolatry of self-sufficiency. "Humble yourselves before the Lord, and he will exalt you" (James 4:10).

Prayer was the breath of the early church. Their poverty and persecution drove them to prayer, while our riches and liberties have busied us so much that we have little time to spare, let alone His burden to bear. A praying church produces passionate evangelists. After their release from the council in Jerusalem, Peter and John met with fellow believers and prayed all the more for boldness to aid them, as they would continue preaching the Word despite the threats they received from the elders (Acts 4:21-29). The result of this fervent prayer was then instantly answered with a mighty shaking and filling of the Spirit, Who clothed them with boldness to evangelize. Who has heard of such a thing in our day?

"In the days of his flesh, Jesus offered up prayers and supplications, with loud cries and tears, to him who was able to save him from death, and he was heard because of his reverence" (Heb. 5:7). Now stamp this verse in your mind as you read the many accounts of our Lord's private prayer life (Matt. 14:23; Mark 1:35; Luke 5:16; Luke 6:12; Luke 22:44). Can you even grasp the idea of how the blessed Son of God prayed with loud cries and reverence as tears gushed out of His holy eyes? During the dark, cold, and lonely hours of the night, as the world slept, the Son of God wept. Can you imagine the Son, Whom all heaven adores, now bowing in soaking wet tears of intercession before the Father on behalf of sinful men? In return, I ask, should not the recipients of this costly intercession thus pray for the many the devil has taken captive to do his will?

I am more sure now than ever that a Christian is only as strong as his prayer life. Heaven recognizes only those prayers that are sincere, reverent, and persistent. The devil fears holy men because holy men are prayerful men, and praying men are God's men. A Christian will be tempted, but he has been granted escape from entering the door of temptation through prayer (1 Cor. 10:13; Matt. 26:41). Without prayer, one will walk right into sin, whereas we will be given wings to fly away from its trap with prayer. Praying for half an hour a week does not make one a prayer warrior. With earnest prayer, one forgets time, gets lost in intercession, and prevails through much wrestling like Jacob, which secures assurance and renders one a warrior before God and a foe before the devil.

After attending many prayer meetings, I realized that the atmosphere in many of these gatherings showed no concern for the Word of the Lord or His presence. Based on the conversations, I can only liken it to a therapy session for building one's self-esteem and confidence. I have had the privilege, should I say, of attending these clubs before. The predictable hour-long meetings were usually accompanied by fifteen minutes of eating and thirty minutes of talking about unfitting matters for saints.

The gatherings were typically finished by giving God the remainder of our fifteen minutes to pray for our physical and material needs. I cannot recall a time when I heard a single individual pray in agony for souls, nor do I ever remember seeing a single teardrop over God's brokenness for sinners. The most frequently used words were "bless us," which essentially translated to, "Lord, keep providing everything my heart desires." Regrettably, it also meant, "Let us remain as we are—tearless, prayerless, burdenless, and passionless. Thank you."

Will such a meeting cause any man's voice to be heard on high? The submission and fear displayed by devils are more discernible to God than those who claim to walk in the light, even as He is in the light.

If God stayed His wrath over a faithless nation because of one man's intercession, even Moses (Num. 14:20), how much more will He arise to show mercy to the souls dangling over the lake of fire through the effectual fervent prayer of the saints? "The LORD is near to all who call on Him in truth" (Psalm 145:18). Many do call on the Lord but to no avail because the calling is not in truth (Prov. 28:9). The world comes running at the opportunity to send their condolences and prayers in response to a tragedy. Although I understand that the statement is meant to show one's level of sympathy, I still ask, to whom are they directing their prayers, especially those devoted to various other religions?

Muslims, Hindus, Buddhists, Daoists, and other religions would like to think of themselves as a praying group of people. So what distinguishes the Christian's prayer from theirs? The Christian's prayer is accepted by way of relationship, whereas the prayers of others never reach the throne room due to their idolatry. Prayers that reach the very altar of incense before the throne are those born in agony. A prayer of intercession is an agony session before God for the souls of men. This type of prayer is oftentimes wordless due to its inexpressible burden, like that of Hannah's before Eli (1 Sam. 1:12-15). Such offering-up of one's heart is a sacrifice that God will never despise (Psalm 51:17). But who desires such a costly prayer life? After all, we are more accustomed to comfortable lives of ease.

Heaven will not issue revival without a revived prayer life. God will deal with you before dealing with others through you. To be a teacher of the Word, you must be a student of prayer, where His presence must still you and, in return, His power fill you. Brethren, it is not only important that we pray; how we pray is of the greatest importance.

I recall a service that we attended, where a youth leader stood up to pray for the church's offering by saying, "Hey, God, what's up? Yeah...um, bless this time, bless this offering. Thanks, God." And everybody responded to that prayer with a loud amen. I almost fainted with astonishment.

The lack of fear of God, which is sorely missing in our generation, was evident in this situation. Our Lord Jesus was heard in prayer because of His reverence (Heb. 5:7). Prayer that is lacking in reverence says a lot about one's seriousness toward the things of God. If you are not serious in prayer, God will not take your prayers seriously. Woe to those devoid of reverence. God is to be approached as your Holy Father in Heaven, wholly, otherly, and set apart. We must treat the sanctuary of God with a reverence that far surpasses even that of the priests of the Old Covenant because of the blood that was shed, not of animals but the only Son of God, making the priests of the New Covenant gain access into the Holy of Holies (Heb. 9:12). "Therefore let us be grateful for receiving a kingdom that cannot be shaken, and thus let us offer to God acceptable worship, with reverence and awe, for our God is a consuming fire" (Heb. 12:28-29).

One praying missionary of Tarsus who journeyed over ten thousand miles turned countless souls to righteousness. This man's name was Paul. Without any political, religious, or organizational backing, this man, Paul, turned the world upside down. Many churches have justified spending billions to evangelize with man-made machinery in their attempt to imitate Paul. In contrast, God's way is raising penniless men and turning such into praying missionaries. Just as hunger leads to eating, desire after God leads to praying. No Christian can excuse himself from prayer. Ardent prayers make apostolic preachers (Acts 1:14). Revivals of the past have been purchased not by gold nor silver but through tears of intercessory saints refusing to accept release from their souls' burden in prayer that they may see sons and daughters rise to a better life.

We have no lack of entertainers, motivational speakers, and self-help gurus; for our pulpits are filled with such. Though these men may fill seats, oftentimes, they do not preach messages that convict the heart and thus populate Heaven with repentant souls. However, men who choose to suffer in intercession to rid souls of sin's obsession and lose many from the devil's possession are the needed giants of our day. Unfortunately, the world is not worthy of such men. We will blush in regret, standing before the Judgment Seat, beholding the King in all His glory, and crying out, "Why did I not pray more?"

CHAPTER 7
TAKE HEART

"We rejoice in our sufferings, knowing that suffering produces endurance,
and endurance produces character, and character produces hope, and hope
does not put us to shame, because God's love has been poured into our hearts
through the Holy Spirit who has been given to us."

Romans 5:3-5

AS A CHRISTIAN, SUFFERING IS inevitable. Thus, we are not to expect fair and cozy treatment from the world. Let us remember in the words of our Lord Jesus Christ, "'A servant is not greater than his master.' If they persecuted me, they will also persecute you" (John 15:20). And, "'If they have called the master of the house Beelzebul, how much more will they malign those of his household'" (Matt. 10:25).

Oh, Christian, the world cannot hate you, but it hates the One Whose word you love and honor (John 7:7). We are hated because He was hated first; and now that He lives in us, we are also hated (John 15:18). The world is not to be considered our friend, nor are we to befriend it.

Contrary to what many preachers would like you to believe, our perfect portion is not in this life. Persecution is welcomed the moment you become a Christian. You become an instant target of the devil because he now views his former soldier as a traitor deserving all of Hell's wrath. The greatest threat to the kingdom of darkness is a Christian who, in his loyalty to God, regards not his life as precious but gives it away as an offering. Such men are not affected by creaturely threats nor wrath, for it is no longer they who live but Christ in them.

The suffering Church throws off all dependency from man and puts it upon God. Only God can help them, or else, they remain helpless. For a child of God, suffering is not seen as a sign of His displeasure but, rather, His good pleasure. For your Father in Heaven, suffering is used to wean you from self-reliance and build such refined trust in His invisible hand, which is ever near and comforting to those who lean upon it. Furthermore, even the apostle Paul and his companions went through such tough times that they often felt as though they had received the sentence of death due to their indescribable afflictions, which they experienced in their missionary venture.

Moreso, what was God trying to show through Paul's suffering? Paul answers, "That was to make us rely not on ourselves but on God who raises the dead" (2 Cor. 1:8-10). From being a persecutor and then into being persecuted, Paul never shied from speaking about his sufferings as a Christian. He was not ashamed of it; nor did he hide it from the churches, which brought encouragement and boldness to them (Phil. 1:14). In fact, this man's introduction to Christianity came with a call to suffer for Christ's name, as he would be shown just how much he would suffer as a chosen instrument to carry Christ's name to the nations (Acts 9:15-16).

For example, Paul's preaching was so bold and controversial that on one occasion, he was stoned so brutally that his assailants were sure he was dead and threw his body outside of the city. However, he was still alive. And believe it or not, when he regained consciousness, he got up and walked right back into the city where the people had tried to kill him.

After revisiting the city, he proclaimed the following to the believers in it: "Through many tribulations we must enter the kingdom of God" (Acts 14:22). The preaching of righteousness cost Paul and Silas public humiliation and even bloody blows with rods, to which they responded with praying and singing. This later resulted in God's mighty power clothing souls with salvation (Acts

16:16-34). As can be seen, Paul's journeys were filled with suffering from imprisonments, countless beatings, many near-death experiences, and the list goes on (2 Cor. 11:23-29). With that in mind, what was it that motivated Paul to press on with such passion and rigor to keep preaching the gospel to a world that was so hostile to its message?

Faith was what motivated Paul to preach the name of Christ, even in the face of death. But unfortunately, it came in the form of his Jewish brethren, screaming in hatred as they held stones in their hands, murder blazing in their eyes. However, one must be controlled with something beyond himself to have such steadfast and unwavering commitment in such dire circumstances—nay, but rather by Someone. This Someone is named Jesus Christ. "For the love of Christ controls us, because we have concluded this: that one has died for all, therefore all have died" (2 Cor. 5:14). The risen Christ living in a crucified Christian makes sufferers rejoice because their suffering produces Christ's endurance, which produces Christ's character; and that character begets the unbreakable assurance of Christ's work of salvation in the soul. Thus, Paul started his new life as a Christian, embracing the narrow path of suffering until the very end. For eventually, Paul would even lay his very life down before Emperor Nero; and as he was beheaded to Rome's wrath, Heaven rejoiced as it welcomed another precious saint home to the loving arms of the Lord.

Martyrdom, while it may not be promised to every Christian, is nonetheless promised to some. Concerning this, the Bible says, "'You will be delivered up even by parents and brothers and relatives and friends, and some of you they will put to death'" (Luke 21:16). We have read and heard of staggering numbers of our precious brothers and sisters being slaughtered throughout the world for worshiping the One Who gave His all for their salvation. Not a drop of their blood will go unnoticed, for "precious in the sight of the Lord is the death of his saints" (Psalm 116:15).

Have we also forgotten the cry of the martyrs who stand before the altar, proclaiming, "'O Sovereign Lord, holy and true, how long before you will judge and avenge our blood on those who dwell on the earth?'" And the response from the heavenly courts will be, "Then they were each given a white robe and told to rest a little longer, until the number of their fellow servants and their brothers should be complete, who were to be killed as they themselves had been" (Rev. 6:9-11). The Son of God's pure robes of righteousness clothe those who had their blood spilled while proclaiming His blood that now keeps them unstained for all eternity. They are comforted and told to rest as their importunate prayer for vengeance will find its fulfillment upon the arrival of the total number of their fellow martyrs.

Tragically, martyrdom will continue to fill the earth with the precious blood of the saints until the time of vengeance arrives. But is this a new concept to our Christian faith? No. Throughout the ages, many have sealed up their testimony with their blood. All eleven apostles, except John, were martyred. Why? For keeping their faith to themselves? Nay, for proclaiming the uncontainable gospel of the Son of God.

I have heard many say that the cross was an instrument of death back in Roman times. Was? It still is. You must die on the cross before experiencing its glorious life. As Christ Himself uttered, "'Truly, truly, I say to you, unless a grain of wheat falls into the earth and dies, it remains alone; but if it dies, it bears much fruit'" (John 12:24). Our Lord Jesus endured the spilling of His blood as He hung on the cross of Calvary to accomplish our salvation. His servants are now called to display the worthiness of that flow by offering their lives to God, even to the point of death.

Likewise, a true martyr's heart is born when the glory of immortality fills the soul, which no longer counts this life of any value nor as precious (Acts 20:24). I daresay that self-preservation has aborted more missionary calls this year alone than all the devilish clinics that have killed precious babies. No one can make the name of Christ known without suffering in some shape or form. God's mark of approval is upon a Christian who suffers for the gospel. "If you are insulted for the name of Christ, you are blessed, because the Spirit of glory and of God rests upon you. But let none of you suffer as a murderer or a thief or an evildoer or as a meddler. Yet if anyone suffers as a Christian, let him not be ashamed, but let him glorify God in that name" (1 Peter 4:14-16). As Jesus said, "'Blessed are those who are persecuted for righteousness' sake, for theirs is the kingdom of heaven. Blessed are you when others revile you and persecute you and utter all kinds of evil against you falsely on my account. Rejoice and be glad, for your reward is great in heaven, for so they persecuted the prophets who were before you'" (Matt. 5:10-12).

We can endure suffering with rejoicing and gladness because of the reward that awaits us; and at the pinnacle of it all, as the prize, is the Father's good pleasure. No matter the depth of our suffering, let us rejoice, be glad, and consider it an honor. As it is written in the Book of Acts, "And when they had called in the apostles, they beat them and charged them not to speak in the name of Jesus, and let them go. Then they left the presence of the council, rejoicing that they were counted worthy to suffer dishonor for the name" (Acts 5:40-41). Contrary to earthly reason, when the precious name of the Son of God is proclaimed at the expense of one's life and reputation, dishonor is a badge of glory.

The life of a follower of the One true God is anything but ordinary. It is the most extraordinary journey possible on this side of eternity, one that is filled with peril. "Many are the afflictions of the righteous, but the LORD delivers him out of them all" (Psalm 34:19). Saints throughout the ages have tasted the power of God's deliverance in different ways:

> Some were tortured, refusing to accept release, so that they might rise again to a better life. Others suffered mocking and flogging, and even chains and imprisonment. They were stoned, they were sawn in two, they were killed with the sword. They went about in skins of sheep and goats, destitute, afflicted, mistreated—of whom the world was not worthy—wandering about in deserts and mountains, and in dens and caves of the earth" (Heb. 11:35-38).

Some were delivered from death, while others went through it. The greatest of saints were the greatest of sufferers. They surely would not have made it to the cover of *Time Magazine* as some preachers, but their worshipful lives made it to the pen of the Holy Spirit. Those who don't make much of themselves while living need not fear, for God can make much more of their lives should they die for His sake. "Therefore let those who suffer according to God's will entrust their souls to a faithful Creator while doing good" (1 Peter 4:19).

If a fire is the best way to purify gold, then a trial is the best way to cleanse a Christian who is more precious to God than any other element in existence. In our trials, we are given eyes to behold our frailty as creatures of dust, by which our dependency on God reaches great heights as never thought possible before. The heat in the furnace gets turned up as all your hidden impurities are burned up until nothing remains except the image of the refining Son. We have reason to rejoice because God's heart is expressed here behind a Christian's trial. "For you know that the testing of your faith produces steadfastness. And let steadfastness have its full effect, that you may be perfect and complete, lacking in nothing" (James 1:3-4). Consider it a gift bestowed upon you by God Himself (Phil. 1:29).

No matter how great our sufferings appear, we must look at them with eyes of faith, believing in the glory that awaits. "For this light momentary affliction is preparing for us an eternal weight of glory beyond all comparison, as we look not to the things that are seen but to the things that are unseen. For the things that are seen are transient, but the things that are unseen are eternal" (2 Cor. 4:17-18). Oh, precious brothers and sisters, let us view our afflictions in light of eternity; then shall joy replace the sorrow of suffering. Indignantly and sorrowfully, we are now witnessing the world suffering from a disease that speaks a different gospel.

We face an epidemic of preachers worldwide, promising their congregations a life free of suffering but filled with riches and good health. This is a life that can be acquired if you satisfy the preacher's wallet. These are men who cry peace when they have something to eat but declare war against those who put nothing into their mouths (Micah 3:5). When offered money to purchase the power of the Spirit by Simon the magician, Peter replied, "'May your silver perish with you, because you thought you could obtain the gift of God with money'" (Acts 8:20). And yet we have thousands of televangelists in America alone, who through their cunning and crafty schemes bewitch the masses into purchasing the Spirit's power, gifts, and graces, as though they were obtainable through perishable means. To the preacher found offering the Spirit's priceless anointing in exchange for the world's perishables, Heaven denounces and warns you sternly by saying, according to Peter, "'You have neither part nor lot in this matter, for your heart is not right before God. Repent, therefore, of this wickedness of yours, and pray to the Lord that, if possible, the intent of your heart may be forgiven you. For I see that you are in the gall of bitterness and in the bond of iniquity'" (Acts 8:21-23).

As a result of salvation, one can now become happy, healthy, and wealthy—or so say many preachers. If this were true, the Bible would say things like, "With enough faith, God will bring all the carnal desires of your heart to fruition." Thankfully, the precious Word of the Lord does not contain any disgusting words like these! If material gains were the marks of true conversion, the Church, which was founded in poverty and persecution, would be considered a failure as it did not meet the prosperous gains that the false prosperity gospel propagates.

Did you know that Christ still suffers over a church that looks no different than the very thing He died to save her from—the world? These are evil times, as many Balaam-like preachers with an appetite for unrighteous wealth have crept into many pulpits. A precious brother from Kenya told me many stories of such preachers who, in the name of prosperity, health, and security, are robbing the poorest in the land. For as the Bible says, "You eat the fat, you clothe yourselves with the wool, you slaughter the fat ones, but you do not feed the sheep. The weak you have not strengthened, the sick you have not healed, the injured you have not bound up, the strayed you have not brought back, the lost you have not sought, and with force and harshness you have ruled them" (Ezek. 34:3-4).

Many people flock to hear such babblers talk about the blessings of materialism; while the masses are sadly and blindly giving away everything from their houses, cars, and even food to obtain the preacher's wish list. This has led millions to file for bankruptcy; and the result is homelessness for many, while the preacher is found sumptuously feeding himself with the blood money. You are not accepted before God because of your social and financial background. You are accepted before God because Christ Jesus died for you, even for your sins. However, because of ill-motived preachers, the message of salvation gets blasphemed by the unbelieving world; and sadly, even the true blessings of godly prosperity are shunned.

God takes utmost delight in prospering His people, and He chooses to use both spiritual and material means to do so. The former is of immeasurable worth, as it opens the door to the latter—as we see with the cases of Abraham, Isaac, Jacob, Joseph, Job, and many others. It is the condition of one's heart, whether their blessings cause the heart to overflow in generosity or lead one to say, "'Soul, you have ample goods laid up for many years; relax, eat, drink, be merry'" (Luke 12:19). "Godliness with contentment is great gain" (1 Tim. 6:6), but the desire for more leaves room for greed. "'They are choked by the cares and riches and pleasures of life, and their fruit does not mature'" (Luke 8:14). "And he said to them, 'Take care, and be on your guard against all covetousness, for one's life does not consist in the abundance of his possessions'" (Luke 12:15). Let God be the One to overflow your cup as you remain steadfast in prioritizing your seeking (Matt. 6:33).

But as for me, oh God, "Two things I ask of you; deny them not to me before I die: Remove far from me falsehood and lying; give me neither poverty nor riches; feed me with the food that is needful for me, lest I be full and deny you and say, 'Who is the LORD?' or lest I be poor and steal and profane the name of my God" (Prov. 30:7-9).

Evil does reign in this fallen world. However, what was intended for evil, God can use for good to further spread the gospel of Christ. Not even the fire of persecution can stop the spread of the gospel. Rather, its enemies are the oil that helps set it ablaze. After Steven's martyrdom (Acts 7:58-60), a great and violent persecution arose against the Church, which drove many believers from Jerusalem to other nations. The Church then moved forward, preaching and suffering as they traveled. As they proclaimed the name of Jesus, God worked salvation in their midst.

As acceptance and redemption resulted from their preaching, so did perilous persecution. That which was designed to extinguish the lamp of the early church only served as an instrument for spreading its flame. Persecution is a tester of genuineness. It is used as God's alarm clock to awaken the slumbering sheep, as a revealer of Judas-like traitors, as well as serving as a preserver and purifier of the faithful. It brings God's most profound comfort to the suffering sheep (2 Cor. 1:5).

It also removes the plague of faithlessness among the sinning goats, who try their best to blend in with the sheep. Its intensity gives a man what comfort and ease cannot, deep and lasting unity. Our safety-embracing and risk-assessing Christian organizations would surely blush in embarrassment should the humble Paul pay a visit in his old, beat-up, and bruised body. Persecution is promised to those who desire to live a godly life (2 Tim. 3:12). Therefore, many fall away due to the cost. These people can be likened to the seed that fell on the rock, who immediately receive it with joy upon hearing the Word but have no root in themselves. They endure for a while; and when tribulation or persecution arises on account of the Word, they immediately fall away (Luke 13:20-21). In other words, persecution is God's way of separating a doer of the Word from a mere hearer of it (James 1:25).

I pray that God, in His mercy, would come and awaken the indifferent and prosperous Laodicea-like church, to see how wretched, pitiable, poor, blind, and naked she has become. We have forgotten the Lord of true riches, clothing, and vision: Jesus Christ. Forgive us, oh, Lord, for preserving the life that you call us to lay down.

CHAPTER 8

THE LIVING WORD

"For the Word of God is living and active, sharper than any two-edged sword, piercing to the division of soul and of spirit, of joints and of marrow, and discerning the thoughts and intentions of the heart."

Hebrews 4:12

FROM THE CAMPS, SLUMPS, AND dungeons of North Korea, Afghanistan, Somalia, Libya, Pakistan, Eritrea, Yemen, Iran, Nigeria, India, and other nations, come the groans of saints. Amid the pain of persecution, they long to drink just one soothing drop of His quenching promise, to comfort their hotly persecuted souls. Truly, these brethren treasure the words of His mouth more than their daily portion of food. Meanwhile, western believers have safe access to both physical and electronic versions of the Bible and virtually no threat of death for believing in the name of Christ. Conversely, it is astounding how much endless travel and depths of suffering believers have endured to acquire even one copy of the sacred Word of God.

On the other hand, we are aliens to such sacrifice because, for most of us, it was and still is just an ordinary book. One that can be easily bought at stores, read at home, and stored up in a bookshelf. Tragically, it has become a book used by some preachers for one hour of stand-up comedy sessions. The saints in distant lands suffer in their pursuit to know God more, and we suffer from too much knowledge. We explain away the Bible's simple call to faith and obedience with unnecessary scholarly rhetoric. To us, it is just another book to be studied but seldom applied practically in our lives. We will do well to remind ourselves that the Bible is anything but an ordinary book. Saints have spilled a sea of righteous blood in the proclamation and preservation of it. They drained out their lifeblood to secure it for the coming generation, whereas we are still debating its validity.

Unlike other books, the Bible is living and active. God Himself inspired holy men to pen it down as they were moved by His Spirit (2 Peter 1:21). The Word of God leads us to God Himself. Whoever uses the Word to draw you away from God is a deceiver who is deceived. After visiting hundreds of churches in the United States, I have noticed that most are not preaching directly from the Bible but around it, with only a handful faithfully preaching from the Word itself. We are facing a faith crisis in our churches mainly because preachers trust in their eloquence to break the invisible chains of sin instead of relying on the Living Word, which is likened to a hammer that breaks the stony heart of a sinner into pieces (Jer. 23:29).

An effective Christian lets the Word take complete possession within them. The indwelling of such a kind will crucify every intellectual boasting within one, and by the Spirit, their soul will cry out the words of the apostle Paul:

> And I, when I came to you, brothers, did not come proclaiming to you the testimony of God with lofty speech or wisdom. For I decided to know nothing among you except Jesus Christ and him crucified. And I was with you in weakness and in fear and much trembling, and my speech and my message were not in plausible words of wisdom, but in demonstration of the Spirit and of power, so that your faith might not rest in the wisdom of men but in the power of God (1 Cor. 2:1-5).

We have a famine of Bible-believing Christians in the land. There are believers who read the Word but rarely any who actively feed on the Word. While many call themselves teachers of the Word, how many allow the Word to teach them? I believe the most dangerous breed of people who become an instant target of the world and the devil are those whose faith runs unto swift obedience. In order for this to be fulfilled, one needs faith. After all, one cannot obey that which he has not believed. Unfortunately, spiritual apathy has possessed many souls, affecting both youths and adults alike. Children and adults alike are more in tune with sports than they are with the will of God, forgetting that whoever and whatever has the heart has you. You love that which you think and talk about the most.

You cannot say that you love God when He is nowhere to be found in your speech, actions, thoughts, and above all, heart. Furthermore, the cherry-picking and choosing of scriptures is an ongoing trend in our churches. Preachers would do well to remember these words of our Lord: "whoever is ashamed of me and my words, of him will the Son of Man be ashamed" (Luke 9:26). Such preachers should repent for shrinking from declaring the whole counsel of God (Acts 20:27). No one can love the Lord Jesus Christ while despising His Word. He is the Word of God which "became flesh and dwelt among us" (John 1:14) "and the name by which he is called is The Word of God" (Rev. 19:13).

The Word Himself highly spoke of the scriptures and always referenced what was written. Thus, the gospel accounts are filled with "have you not read" statements. Still, the precious Word of God is taken for granted when countless hours are spent debating its authenticity instead of believing the truth that it communicates. My heart is anguished after reading many accounts of precious Christians in North Korea meeting in cramped sewers to petition God for a copy of the Bible while fearful of being caught by their persecutors, all the while jubilant and flowing in tearful thanksgiving. Meanwhile, attending million-dollar venues with no shortages of Bibles and fingerprints on their pages, I blush at our boasted freedoms and comforts, which have bound many in chains of ungratefulness as they fail to acknowledge the precious Word that lies at their disposal.

We can't handle such fiery faith of our brothers from persecuted nations. What we call fanaticism, they call faith, and what we describe as legalism, they describe as obedience. The difference is that their simple faith leads to passionate obedience, while our intellectual faith leads to endless debates that risk talking one out of it. Faith comes from hearing and hearing through the Word of Christ. I am not asking you to move to North Korea or even China, but I am pleading for hearts to be clothed with childlike and single-minded obedience to the glory of God. As a newborn desires the mother's milk, a believer must desire the Word of God by which he grows in maturity. As the Word says, "Like newborn infants, long for the pure spiritual milk, that by it you may grow up into salvation—" (1 Peter 2:2). The Word of God is our defense and offense, and to use it properly, you must bring it out in a timely manner, lest the schemes of the evil one swallow you up.

"Whoever is of God hears the words of God. The reason why you do not hear them is that you are not of God" (John 8:47) and the hearing that results in doing brings blessing: "Blessed rather are those who hear the word of God and keep it" (Luke 11:28)! There is a great searching for the anointing of the Spirit in today's churches and conferences. But alas, we are looking for it in all the wrong places when the blessing has been placed at the Church's doorstep all along—the Word of God—when read humbly and prayerfully: "He leads the humble in what is right, and teaches the humble his way" (Psalm 25:9).

Father of the fatherless and protector of widows is God in His holy habitation. He is the One who upholds the universe by the Word of His power, hangs the earth on nothing, and makes the clouds rise at the ends of the earth, the least of them weighing over a million pounds. He also makes lightning for the rain and brings forth the wind from His storehouses. Furthermore, He raises the poor from the dust, lifts the needy from the ash heap, dwells in the high and holy place, and also is with him who is of a contrite and lowly spirit, and revitalizes the spirit of the lowly, and revives the heart of the contrite.

After such majestic descriptions of the power of His Word and character, are we quickly swayed by unbelieving lips which would have us think of the Word of God as no different than any other book? "Nay, let God be true though everyone were a liar." Therefore, an unbeliever can read the Bible all they want to no avail, for pride blinds them to what only humility can open their eyes to. So, one should be cautious not to harden their hearts to the conviction of the Lord. For the life that the Lord provides is of overflowing spiritual abundance (Job 26:7; Heb. 1:3; Psalm 135:7; Psalm 113:7; Isa. 57:15; Psalm 68:5; Rom. 3:4).

"Did God actually say, 'You shall not eat of any tree in the garden?'" asked the devil pretentiously to Eve. Well-knowing the command of God, she replied, "We may eat of the fruit of the trees in the garden, but God said, 'You shall not eat of the fruit of the tree that is in the midst of the garden, neither shall you touch it, lest you die.'"

"'You will not surely die,'" the serpent said to the woman (Gen. 3:1-4). Let us revisit chapter two of the Book of Genesis, where God strictly charged the man, saying, "'You may surely eat of every tree of the garden, but of the tree of the knowledge of good and evil you shall not eat, for in the day that you eat of it you shall surely die.'"

We learn that the devil has been in the business of turning God's don'ts into do's from the very beginning. On the one hand, death is decreed, and on the other hand, death is nullified. God's simple command reads, "You shall surely die," while the foe would like to whisper in this manner, "Let me retranslate that verse for you; the words cannot be taken literally as they appear. God doesn't actually mean what He says, so we have to tweak, turn, or even remove some words that conflict with our natural desires, hindering us from achieving God-like illumination. God surely does understand your pursuit of these fulfilling lusts." Now, imagine the devil's role as an influencer for our modern-day faithless Bible readers, debaters, scholars, and even preachers who quickly suppress supernatural or costly occurrences in the scriptures. They shun it as non-applicable to their reality or drag it down to the level of natural phenomenon, robbing God of His full glory. The tempter lies to many with deceptive words that promise life at the beginning of one's blind pursuit of sin but lead to the bitter sentence of death in the end. As

God's Word says, "There is a way that seems right to a man, but its end is the way of death" (Prov. 14:12).

The answer for the present and future generations is to be found in the incorruptible and infallible Word of God. It has suffered much under Empires, Monarchies, and Tyrants who wished its extinction. Yet unharmed, it stood triumphantly beside their grave. Where are those who, in their raging fury, tried to outlive and outdo its influence? Even as the words which the Lord commanded the prophets overtook the disobedient fathers during Zechariah's time, in the same way, the Word of God overtook and continues to surpass all those who desire its destruction. Their fleeting life, along with their accomplishments, is brought to naught as it perishes from under the earth.

But praise be to God! His Word flourishes still as it treads over the dirt of its persecutors. No flesh can touch, let alone destroy that which is eternal and forever firmly fixed in the heavens (Psalm 119:89). Since God Himself has promised us regarding the immortality of His promises, let us hold fast to them (Isa. 40:8; Luke 21:33). Therefore, pick up the Ancient Book, shake off its dust and humbly study it. Allow it to teach, reproof, correct, and train you in righteousness that you may be complete and equipped for every good work (2 Tim. 3:16-17).

CHAPTER 9

ETERNITY

*"What is your life? For you are a mist that appears
for a little time and then vanishes."*

James 4:14

ETERNITY MUST BE AT THE forefront of our eyes. The more conscious we are of heavenly treasures, the less we are mesmerized by earthly possessions. We must remind ourselves daily about the brevity of human life. No matter how hard one tries to suppress the thought of the afterlife, the heart will wrestle and circle back with the same reality. Why? It is because "he has put eternity into man's heart" (Eccl. 3:11). The flesh is made from the dust, and to dust, it returns, whereas the soul will live on forever.

Our time on earth is short and cannot be compared to the vastness of eternity. Heaven and hell are only a breath away, and we will do well to remind ourselves to live with their perspective. When we rub off the dust of time from our eyes, we can then clearly behold the present world with the lens of eternity, which will result in the swift crucifixion of worldliness and a revived prayerfulness. Will anyone be able to look into those holy eyes, which are like a flame of fire, and juggle for justification for having talked themselves out of obedience? Were we to be lifted up like Paul and John the Apostle, from time into eternity, whether it be in a vision or a dream and granted surpassing revelations of the age to come, would we ever dream of returning to the corruption of the world? Would we continue to live inside a spiritual refrigerator, frozen and void of passion and pure devotion? Would we still want to enjoy the fleeting pleasures of sin? Would the riches of Egypt sway us, or like Moses, consider the reproach of Christ a treasure of infinite worth?

Marvel at this, the God who inhabits eternity now makes His habitation inside a believing heart. But alas! Many attendees of God's house are unmoved because He does not live in their hearts. The snare of materialism has captured many souls and bound them captive with chains of earthly satisfaction without regard to the eternity to come.

"If then you have been raised with Christ, seek the things that are above, where Christ is, seated at the right hand of God. Set your mind on things that are above, not on things that are on earth. For you have died, and your life is hidden with Christ in God. When Christ who is your life appears, then you also will appear with him in glory" (Col. 3:1-4). A mind that is set on things above will want heavenly riches, but a mind that is set on earth will desire earthly perishables. Why, oh soul, will you labor for earth's best when God has promised you heavenly days of eternal rest? Have you not received the inexpressible riches of His joy that you should go about looking to fill the void with earth's toys? Nothing on this side of eternity can compare with the immeasurable treasures of being in God's presence. Despite knowing the brevity of life, people spend lifetimes pursuing the fading pleasures and riches of the earth only to wake up in hell one day.

> Then I saw a great white throne and him who was seated on it. From his presence earth and sky fled away, and no place was found for them. And I saw the dead, great and small, standing before the throne, and books were opened. Then another book was opened, which is the book of life. And the dead were judged by what was written in the books, according to what they had done. And the sea gave up the dead who were in it, Death and Hades gave up the dead who were in them, and they were judged, each one of them, according to what they had done. Then Death and Hades were thrown into the lake of fire. This is the second death, the lake of

fire. And if anyone's name was not found written in the book of life, he was thrown into the lake of fire (Rev. 20:11-15).

Can any of us envision this coming day in our hearts and still afford to live unto ourselves? Should we not desire the names of our neighbors to be found written in the Lamb's Book of Life? Is the thought of the unbearable heat of the lake of fire still not enough to set your frozen and slumbering heart ablaze and quickened for evangelism? How often does your heart ache with unceasing sorrow at the thought of your father, mother, sister, brother, cousin, or friend being cast into the lake of fire for eternity? Do you not realize that what you sow on earth, you reap in eternity?

You preachers of Babylon, how will you make eye contact with the One whose face shines brighter than the sun and answer for curing lightly the wounds of cancerous disease of spreading sinfulness? Oh, to live the remainder of our fleeting days in light of this glorious and dreadful vision of the future appointment before the One at whose presence the earth trembles and mountains smoke. If the blazing glory of His presence alone makes the creation blush with unworthiness, what do you think we will do when we see Him? John, the beloved apostle of our Lord Jesus, the only one who, according to traditions, was said to have outlived the rest, and on one occasion, was caught up into eternity, was left to rot in an island called Patmos for proclaiming the crucified and risen Lord Jesus Christ. This Jesus that John saw was nothing like the earthly Jesus regarding His bodily appearance. The One who was marred beyond human semblance as He suffered on the cross is now crowned with such great glory and power that upon seeing Him, "clothed with a long robe and with a golden sash around his chest. The hairs of whose head were white, like white wool, like snow. His eyes were like a flame of fire, his feet were like burnished bronze, refined in a furnace, and his voice was like the roar of many waters. In his right hand held seven stars, from his mouth came a sharp two-edged sword, and his face was like the sun shining in full strength (Rev. 1:13-16).

John fell at His feet as though dead. This is an instinctive creaturely reaction to the Holy Creator of all. Believers and unbelievers alike will thus respond to His glorious majesty in this manner. However, the believer will be welcomed with the words, "fear not," whereas an unbeliever, in his dreaded appearance, will hear the roar of these words, "depart from me."

In vain, will many wish to turn the clock backward in hopes of seizing the lost opportunity to believe the gospel when it was first proclaimed to them. The mercy of God is for now, not then. As the apostle Paul says, "Behold, now is the favorable time; behold, now is the day of salvation" (2 Cor. 6:2). Unending days of joy await the righteous, whereas eternal torment awaits the unrighteous. In seven years of residing in the United States, I have not heard one whole sermon on the topic of hell.

Our Lord Jesus talked about hell more than priests, judges, kings, and prophets combined. Not only that, but He painted a very graphic picture of the place with these words, "where their worm does not die and the fire is not quenched" (Mark 9:48). The worm of one's nagging guilty conscience, and the fires of God's wrath are explained in the gospel according to Luke, chapter 16, in the parable of the rich man and Lazarus. Out of the flames, where mercy and comfort are denied him and at the realization of his just verdict, the rich man in his last attempt, begs for an evangelist to be sent to warn the remainder of his family on earth about the terrible nature of this place, called hell (Luke 16:19-31).

Could it be that the hopeless and doomed sinners in hell are more concerned about warning souls regarding everlasting fire than most Christians of our day? One's unbelief does not change the reality of this place. Most preachers have eliminated the topic of hell from their sermons, and the listeners, from their vocabulary. No wonder why many churchgoers find it a subject of contention and debate.

Many people desire Heaven on their own terms, but once the conditions are read, many turn away after realizing that one must believe in Christ alone to receive such an undeserved inheritance. Heaven without God, and the pursuit of self-satisfaction without Hell, are the desires of many. To an unbeliever, Heaven is desirable as long as they see themselves on the throne; whereas a Christian desires Heaven because God is there, and it is not the gold of Heaven that the Christian desires but the God of it. "Making the best use of the time, because the days are evil" (Eph. 5:16).

We had better use our time with eternity's values in view. Just in the past hour alone, thousands of people perished, and how many do you suppose made it into His bosom while the rest were cast into the outer darkness, weeping and gnashing their teeth? The narrow and true way has many hardships, but the promise of glory waits at the end. "will those who are saved be few?" asked someone, to which the Lord replied, "Strive to enter through the narrow door. For many, I tell you, will seek to enter and will not be able" (Luke 13:23-24). Yes, is the Lord's answer to the question. The wide path is an easy path that appeals to the unconverted eye while luring the heart to enter the direction of its selfish cravings, which leads to damnation. Cruise right along and do absolutely nothing, says the signboard on the wide gate, whereas the signs on the narrow gate read, "This is the way, walk in it" (Isa. 30:21).

"For the things that are seen are transient, but the things that are unseen are eternal" (2 Cor. 4:18). After having the Damascus Road experience with the Lord Jesus Christ, I believe the apostle Paul did not merely become a good man but a heavenly man with heavenly desires. With an ardent pursuit of the Lord, this man became eternity conscious, the fruit of which we see in his immediate and urgent evangelism following baptism. He was very aware of the innumerable souls who would one day stand before the judgment seat of Christ to be judged for their deeds, and his dread of the Lord over this day fueled his evangelism and put eternity before his eyelids (2 Cor. 5:10-11).

When waking and sleeping, there is one portion of the Psalms that will roll back the curtain of time from our earthly eyes and set them upon eternity, let us pray and live considering these words: "O LORD, make me know my end and what is the measure of my days; let me know how fleeting I am! Behold, you have made my days a few handbreadths, and my lifetime is as nothing before you. Surely all mankind stands as a mere breath! *Selah* Surely a man goes about as a shadow! Surely for nothing they are in turmoil; man heaps up wealth and does not know who will gather" (Psalm 39:4-6).

The Old Testament saints like Daniel in particular, were given visions and shown the great and terrible day of the Lord. Here is how Daniel describes this glorious yet terrifying vision: "As I looked, thrones were placed, and the Ancient of Days took his seat; his clothing was white as snow, and the hair of his head like pure wool; his throne was fiery flames; its wheels were burning fire. A stream of fire issued and came out from before him; a thousand thousands served him, and ten thousand times ten thousand stood before him; the court sat in judgment, and the books were opened" (Dan. 7:9-10).

This same glorified Jesus Christ that John accounts beholding in eternity, at whose presence he fell as though dead, is seen by Daniel. And as Daniel is given an interpretation of the authority of Christ over nations and kings, he states, "As for me, Daniel, my thoughts greatly alarmed me, and my color changed, but I kept the matter in my heart" (Dan. 7:28). Can you imagine what must have gone through the corridors of this man's mind after seeing that glorious picture of eternity and the judgment seat at that? I believe Daniel's heart grew more in touch with the realms of eternity after that experience.

I appeal to you, oh preacher, by the shortness of time, to return preaching about heaven and hell even at the expense of your popularity. Preach heaven in such a way as to make people feel caught up in the glory of it and preach hell in a manner where they can smell the smoke and feel the burning terrors of it. Preach with your eyes upon the judgment seat, not the pew. While you are sure to get dismissed as one who has lost all sanity, you would have secured the eternity of those with eyes to see and ears to hear. Keep the glories of Heaven in your right eye and the torments of Hell in the left and preach through the lens of those realities.

So, tell me, why are you preaching if not for the Lord's glory? Do you believe in an actual Heaven? Do you believe in an actual Hell? Can you see the chasm fixed between the two places, where one cannot cross to extend mercy, and the other cannot beg enough for it? There is not a soul on earth who will not become an effective evangelist for the kingdom of God when mindful of these truths. You cannot be urgent about someone else's eternal state when your own is gravely neglected.

Can one believe in Heaven and live as though they were never going there, and can one believe in Hell and fail to warn those on their way there? No! Standing before the throne while the books are opened and accounts are read, I believe the greatest of all embarrassments will be felt by preachers who, in the name of love and tolerance, withheld the weightier matters of the gospel, namely the judgment of sinners. They will have to witness scores of their unconverted recipients accuse them of hiding the truth and blinding their souls with false assurances which promised salvation, only to realize their looming damnation at hand. The preachers can only wish to go back in time and crucify these eternity-costing loopholes brought about by their preachings. Let the following words not be prayed on that day: "Had I dug up the words of His warnings as precious stones from under the earth, instead of choosing the surface-level of understanding which my heart afforded, I would have been spared from witnessing the hay, wood and stubble-like work, which my wisdom founded, go up in flames of His testing" (1 Cor. 3:12-15, paraphrase).

To spare preachers the blush of that awful sight, I plead that we repent from where we have fallen and beg to have the veils of time removed and see our passing lives through eternity's binoculars. One millisecond in Hell will awaken and equip the preacher of this generation with the urgency and fervency of the prophets and apostles. Intoxication to entertainment and love for material possessions have blinded many eyes to the vision of eternity and deafened ears to the shout of the trumpet call, "Prepare to meet thy God." I don't believe awakening will come until God, in His great mercy, strips us of everything that we have been leaning upon for far too long. Oh, that God would remove the lid from our spiritualized vocabularies which appear reasonable in speech but are veiled by desires to serve the flesh. I pray that He will shower us with Spirit-birthed repentance and revive the Church's concern for the eternal abode of the Christ-less multitudes.

Every second, minute, hour, and day pushes us closer to eternity. This frail and wasting form that we call our earthly bodies will at any time put off mortality and be clothed with immortality. Whichever way we exit out of this world, we must all appear before the judgment seat of Christ, which will dictate one's eternal destiny. Fear not death, rather him who, "'after he has killed, has authority to cast into hell. Yes, I tell you, fear him'" (Luke 12:5). Let us remember that our Lord has conquered death, and "'I have the keys of Death and Hades'" (Rev. 1:18). While nothing can separate the believer from the love of God in Christ Jesus, in the same way, nothing can free the sinner from God's wrath except for the one man, Christ Jesus.

"Such appeal to conversion is based on fear and unbecoming of the Christ we know from the gospels," say those who are fantasizing about a man whose nature looks awfully like theirs rather than the One, who is coming "in flaming fire, inflicting vengeance on those who do not know God and on those who do not obey the gospel of our Lord Jesus" (2 Thess. 1:8). He will always be gentle and meek only to those who desire to see with a humble plea because "with the merciful you show yourself merciful; with the blameless man you show yourself blameless; with the purified you show yourself pure; and with the crooked you make yourself seem tortuous. For you save a humble people, but the haughty eyes you bring down" (Psalm 18:25-27).

"All the paths of the LORD are steadfast love and faithfulness, for those who keep his covenant and his testimonies" (Psalm 25:10). The gentle and meek Lord who "went about doing good and healing all who were oppressed by the devil" during His first coming is the same One, at Whose second coming, the enemies of the gospel are found begging mountains and rocks with these words, "Fall on us and hide us from the face of him who is seated on the throne, and from the wrath of the Lamb" (Rev. 6:16). The crucified Christ of Calvary will not judge you, rather the risen Christ of eternity. The former died to save, the latter lives to judge.

There is a great focus on the kindness of Christ but hardly any mention of Christ's severity. Oh, Christian, you have an eternity of righteousness, joy, and peace to look forward to. Therefore, will you not desire to be made poor in spirit to make the unrighteous rich in faith? Should not your eyes shed streams of sorrowful tears so that sinners can offer joyful, salvific prayers? Can you not endure some sleepless nights in intercession, in hopes of awakening an interest in the sinner's heart for the Savior's blood? "Behold, he is coming with the clouds, and every eye will see him, even those who pierced him, and all tribes of the earth will wail on account of him. Even so. Amen" (Rev. 1:7). May God Almighty keep our eyes transfixed upon eternity.

Know ye not, the curtain of time will soon give way,

The judgment seat of Christ, where summons the Potter His clay.

Every idle word, every secret deed, the light shall display;

Eternal throne of God, may our eyes never betray,

Can you look into those eyes, ablaze with holiness,

He will require from your life the fruit of godliness;

As you stand there in awe, beholding His worthiness,

Blush you will, trading His presence for fleeting happiness.

What answer should you give Him, for time has now stopped,

Your verdict will be final and eternity sealed, the gavel has been dropped;

Acknowledge then your frailty, and run to Him who holds immortality,

For why should you perish when the gift is freely offered by Him who inhabits eternity.

CHAPTER 10

REST ASSURED

"And he said to them, 'Come away by yourselves
to a desolate place and rest a while.'"

Mark 6:31

THE MOST PROFOUND SOURCE OF comfort for a weary pilgrim is to know the great depths of the love of God with which he is loved. The love of God can be likened to a cold drop of water to a pilgrim stranded in the desert of discouragement. Its assurance reaches down to the inner man, quenching the panting after God's comfort, which then strengthens the heart in faith and produces confidence of Christ's indwelling in the soul. A man who does the work of the Lord without the love of the Lord will surely dehydrate his inward man and soon experience symptoms of spiritual fatigue. Without drinking again from the fountain of Christ's quenching love, he will eventually collapse. It is God Who "first loved us" (1 John 4:19). Therefore, His love for us makes our love for Him possible. If you genuinely desire to understand the love of God for you, look no further than the blood-stained cross of our Lord Jesus Christ.

"But God shows his love for us in that while we were still sinners, Christ died for us" (Rom. 5:8). It would have been enough for God to have simply expressed His love through words, which He had, throughout the Old Testament; but He went above and beyond to demonstrate that love by dying. Indeed, "greater love has no one than [Christ]" (John 15:13), Who sacrificially "'la[id] down his life for the sheep'" (John 10:11). Our Lord Jesus has not only secured the salvation of those who believe but also won the glorious assurance of it. We need the assurance of salvation for our endurance; for without it, the tribulation promised to a believer in this life would discourage him from running the race due to overwhelming sorrow of heart. Thus, the glorious vision of the prize at the end of the finish line of faith would be blurred.

What great comfort the soul can experience in knowing that God never leaves His work in a believer unfinished (Phil. 1:6). Confidence in God's faithfulness makes the road ahead endurable, for He has said, "I will never leave you nor forsake you" (Heb. 13:5). God shows great emotion toward the suffering of His people, even the backslidden in heart. In His response to penitent Israel, God says, "Is Ephraim my dear son? Is he my darling child? For as often as I speak against him, I do remember him still. Therefore, my heart yearns for him; I will surely have mercy on him, declares the LORD" (Jer. 31:20). And for a backsliding Israel, here is the Lord's heart: "How can I give you up, O Ephraim? How can I hand you over, O Israel? How can I make you like Admah? How can I treat you like Zeboiim? My heart recoils within me; my compassion grows warm and tender" (Hosea 11:8).

See what depth of compassion God is willing to extend to rebels who are unconcerned about Him. Reflect on how much more He will wrap His arms of compassion around the son and daughter of His delight and walk with them in all the joys and afflictions of this life! Oh, Christian, family may forsake you; your closest friends may turn against you and the world may be repulsed by your very existence; but God, in His unwavering faithfulness, speaks to you in this manner: "Can a woman forget her nursing child, that she should have no compassion on the son of her womb? Even these may forget, yet I will not forget you. Behold, I have engraved you on the palms of my hands; your walls are continually before me" (Isa. 49:15-16). Why should we fear today's trying times and those to come when such precious promises are at our disposal?

Since the ransom of our lives is costly and could never suffice, God had to be the only one to accomplish this great salvation, and to the awe of angels and devils, God took on flesh and walked among us. He lived a sinless life for the sake of our righteousness. He experienced a crushing death to satisfy the wrath of the Father for the sins of the world, thus securing forgiveness for us. His triumphant resurrection completed the work of salvation and redemption, tearing the veil in the holy of holies. The gates of Heaven swung wide open for both Jews and Gentiles through the blood of His cross. Heaven thus proclaims the access to the Father's presence opened to both Jews and Gentiles alike, through the blood of His cross, which has now swung wide open the gates of Heaven for them that believe.

> Therefore, brothers, since we have confidence to enter the holy places by the blood of Jesus, by the new and living way that he opened for us through the curtain, that is, through his flesh, and since we have a great priest over the house of God, let us draw near with a true heart in full assurance of faith, with our hearts sprinkled clean from an evil conscience and our bodies washed with pure water (Heb. 10:19-22).

The Son was treated like a criminal so that criminals would be treated as sons. Bearing your eternal damnation while being hung on that cursed tree to secure your salvation, the Lamb suffered thus to bring you into glory. The destructive outcome of his sin in the garden got the first Adam kicked out of paradise and away from the tree of life. In contrast, the redemptive work of the last Adam has reopened the gates of the garden, granting many sons and daughters to eat of the tree of life in the paradise of God. Sin entered as a result of eating the fruit of Eden's forbidden tree, which brought death to mankind; and now righteousness inhabits many who, by faith, believe in the fruit of Calvary's tree, which gives eternal life to all who believe.

Oh, beloved Christian, you are God's treasured possession, and He deems you righteous, not by your work but by His. The Bridegroom awaits His bride every passing second while the angels anticipate the glory of the coming marriage feast of the Lamb. Put your eyes upon that day, oh pilgrim, and know you are marching to victory despite what you see or hear. "The righteous falls seven times and rises again" (Prov. 24:16); and "though he fall, he shall not be cast headlong, for the LORD upholds his hand" (Psalm 37:24). Oh weary soul, believe what the Lord has said about His unchanging character and see through your transient circumstances with eyes resting upon His mercy. For great is His mercy and well able to deliver you from the roaring waves of despair and uncertainty. God is ever close to the righteous because they are ever dependent on Him. He is always found in their camp, where hearts gather to seek His will. Therefore, knowing the greatness of God's love and the tenderness of His compassion should make the Christian live and die for Calvary's cause alone.

CHAPTER 11

THE NEED SURPASSES ITS WORKERS

"And I heard the voice of the Lord saying, 'Whom shall I send, and who will go for us?' Then I said, 'Here I am! Send me.'"

Isaiah 6:8

MANY PEOPLE COMPLAIN ABOUT EVIL in the world and shake their fists at the heavens. Why is God not doing anything to save people Himself, they wonder? Throughout man's history, God's plan has always been to reunite humanity back to Himself. And since the death and resurrection of our Lord Jesus Christ, God has appointed the work of evangelism to everyone who calls Jesus their Lord. The need to preach the word to a lost sea of people is profound and very distressing when one looks at it through God's weeping eyes. We live in a world where corruption is exalted and honesty is detested. There is no fear of God before those who govern their population except a handful who choose to honor God at the expense of their employment, reputation, and even death. These handfuls are like the Hebrew midwives who chose God's fear over Pharaoh's tyrannical command to annihilate all the male Hebrew children (Exod. 1:16-17). If the growing number of abortion clinics, politicians legislating unrighteousness, drug use plaguing the nation, and the glamorization of sin being plastered throughout your neighborhood do not alarm you, then what will?

Once, we were all enslaved to sin, which could be likened unto the Israelites in Egypt, until God's mercy brought us out from the bondage of slavery into freedom. Having once been slaves, have we forgotten about the millions who are still chained to the pharaohs of our day? Human trafficking comes in different forms, but two of the most prominent ones are through forced labor and prostitution. The blood money of the latter brings in over $99 billion a year in revenue, easily making it the most in-demand service for the devilish corporation profiting over $150 billion a year from exploiting young children, women, and men. What about the millions of children who dwell in the slums of India and Africa that are scrambling for a piece of bread and clothing? They labor tirelessly to simply exist.

Being overcome with depression and to drown out the sorrow of loneliness, we have a staggering rate of people overdosing on pain medications. In 2020 alone, we had over ninety thousand reported deaths in the United States due to drug overdose. Three months before his passing, Mr. William Booth, who founded the Salvation Army, uttered this precious heart cry: "While women weep, as they do now, I'll fight; while children go hungry, as they do now I'll fight; while men go to prison, in and out, in and out, as they do now, I'll fight; while there is a poor lost girl upon the streets, while there remains one dark soul without the light of God, I'll fight, I'll fight to the very end!"[1]

What a powerful cause to declare! Where are the John the Baptists to fight for their nations' declining condition with the gospel of repentance? Where are the William Booths, who, for the drunkards and prostitutes, march the streets proclaiming the gospel of deliverance? Where are the William Wilberforces to fight for the enslaved with the gospel of liberty? Where are the Wesleys who travel the length and breadth of their country to rescue poverty-stricken souls, heralding the gospel of hope? Where are the George Whitefields who preach with tears for the tearless and indifferent sinners

---

1   William Booth, "I'll Fight," The Salvation Army, Accessed July 12, 2025, https://www.salvationarmy.org.au/illfight.

with the gospel of salvation? Where are the C.T. Studds who put down their earthly crowns to clothe the unreached with heavenly riches through the gospel of grace? Where are the Hudson Taylors who examine and cure the sick with the stethoscope of Christ's mercy, leading the coldest of sinners into the warmth of the gospel of love? Where are the Amy Carmichaels, who, with Christ's banner of love, stand up for the rights of the orphans and welcome them into the loving arms of the Heavenly Father by proclaiming the gospel of adoption?

These are but a few names of those who saw the shed blood of the Lamb worthy of all their tears and sacrifice, along with millions who bowed themselves in humility. In due time, they were made to soar through the eternity with the God Who was ever a Father and a friend to them. The saints of the past were left with their generation of sinners, and we are left with ours—and time is closing in on us. What will it take for us to see that what God is looking for is simply a man wholly surrendered to His leading and guidance? God will not grant His power to the unyielded man or woman. Brethren, the only way to victory is to submit to His perfect will.

I have scratched just the surface of the crisis we face in our world today; and for many of us, it is too much to bear, let alone act upon. I have heard many Christians, even some in their old age, state that they would instead focus on the positive and not the negative. I suppose then they would be fine closing their eyes and shutting their ears to the thousands around them headed to perdition while preferring to maintain their sanity. No believer can carry the Lord's joy without His burden; and conversely, they cannot bear His burden without His joy. The fire to speak the gospel has stopped burning in the hearts of many former missionaries, now turned stationaries and evangelists with many great opportunities missed.

"I used to have the fire once," say those whose hearts burn not with the opening of Scriptures as it used to, whose indifference toward the things of God is no different than an unbeliever, whose prayers have not the slightest amount of zeal to pull down strongholds, and whose love for the One Who saved their souls cannot be traced.

"What put out the fire?" I've asked the fireless bunch.

"Life," they say.

If I am reading correctly, I find the older the apostles, the bolder their faith; whereas in our case, the older the person, the colder their aversion. Will you, oh man or woman, rest content in this pitiable form when the open door for cleansing, refilling, and indwelling lies in front of you?

There is mercy for those who acknowledge their bareness in the spirit so that His Spirit can make fruitful the withered areas of the heart. To such a one, God says, "Return, O faithless children, declares the LORD; for I am your master; I will take you, one from a city and two from a family, and I will bring you to Zion" (Jer. 3:14), and "Return, O faithless sons; I will heal your faithlessness." to which I plead, your response would be that of humble repentance: "Behold, we come to you, for you are the LORD our God" (Jer. 3:22).

With Bibles at our fingertips and countless works of Christian literature at our disposal, our generation has been supplied with more truth and light than it knows how to handle. Reminiscing revivals seem to have only moved our intellect and barely our feet. Zeal without knowledge is fire without control, whereas knowledge without zeal is a bunch of refrigerated babble. "Do not be slothful in zeal, be fervent in spirit, serve the Lord" (Rom. 12:11). The need is overwhelming and only piling up by day, and we must see to it; and if the light is put out, how will the darkness be exposed? Oh, why is the Church so sluggish at this crucial hour? Who will awake the sleeping billions who are snoring their way to damnation? Therefore, let us not begin with the question, how can I start, but rather, where can I start?

Years ago, I recalled meeting a greatly respected and well-educated preacher for a word of encouragement. To my utter shock, twenty-five out of the thirty minutes of the meeting were used to boast of the preacher's many degrees and accomplishments that hung on his office wall. The remaining five minutes were used to encourage this needy sheep to attain an education of his stature. Dejected, I walked out of that office, never wishing upon myself an education, the kind that this proud preacher possessed. Numerous other stories can be recalled, but I would spare us all the grief of knowing such men who, although good with words, are devoid of humility. Furthermore, they give off a putrid smell of intellectual pride to believers who simply desire to be at their Lord's humble service.

Soon after my rebirth, I was given a terrifying dream that left its imprint on my inward man, which I am sure will forever remain seared into my soul. In the dream, I was at a three-story home, making my way up the stairs to the third floor, when I suddenly saw a figure that had its back turned toward me. Besides the figure was a temple filled with idols of silver and gold, and incense was offered to most of them. I knew the figure was a woman because it was wearing a red sari; and I realized that this was none other than my grandmother, who had passed away eight years earlier. I walked toward her and gently put my hands on her shoulders to behold her appearance; and upon calling her name, she turned around and beheld me in a lifeless form. Her eyes were blacker than charcoal, and her hair was uncombed with a stare that sent chills down my spine.

Slowly, my feet started moving backward as horror filled my heart with unmentionable pain, which came into being out of sensing the dwelling place of her eternal soul. I called out to her, "Grandmother, Grandmother, it is I, your grandson!"

I was hoping to hear at least a word or two from her lips when, out of nowhere, a voice suddenly spoke. "She is in Hell; now go warn others."

I was overcome with a deep sadness in my soul and started to weep bitterly, wishing I had at least one opportunity to share the gospel with the grandmother I loved and whose lifeless figure stood before me. It was at that very moment that I realized the grief that I felt and the tears that I had shed were unveiling my earthly eyes to the Lord's heart, for those separated from the glory of His might suffer the punishment of eternal torment. With such a dream, the greatest need for evangelization came to the forefront of all my needs; and nothing else would do. Men of courage are needed to bring the rod of the Word to smite the God-defying cultural norms of our day. Living in the midst of a sin-soaked culture, it would even appear as though evil were gaining an edge. But Scripture makes it clear that the darker the world appears, the brighter the illumination of the gospel. Amen.

The present mounting needs are making souls ripe for the harvest. Read through the pages of church history, which clearly show us the soul-saving work of God amidst the vilest of kings, emperors, popes, and governors who exercised ungodliness and plunged their nations to moral, economic, and social ruin through greed for power and wealth. As tragic as it seems, there is yet hope for a mighty harvest, even while corruption reigns; but the Book must be proclaimed by those who have pledged their souls to its Author. "He who gathers in summer is a prudent son, but he who sleeps in harvest is a son who brings shame" (Prov. 10:5).

Often, the Lord's most mighty works begin with the simple. For example, God changes a person before He changes an entire nation. He surgically removes the old heart of rebellion and gives us a new spirit of obedience. Let the emperors, presidents, prime ministers, judges, legislators, and everyone else in positions of power be given this new heart through faith, which will surely result in righteousness, justice, and mercy flowing from their governments. But alas, many continue to reject good and welcome evil to their own demise.

Consider, for example, how God sent Moses to break Pharoah's yoke of slavery, Elijah to confront Ahab's idolatry, Isaiah to preach to a stubborn nation, John the Baptist to wake a slumbering nation, and Paul to evangelize the unreached peoples. With many others throughout history, these men have been the ones to change the hearts of kings, deliver the captives, and reform nations with lasting impact. These remarkable feats were all fulfilled through their simple obedience to the Word of God. I ask, then, what is it that hinders believers today from pursuing such feats?

While man's creativity has advanced prior generations' expectations, the heart remains desperately wicked and beyond human help. As blind and hardened as sinners are, there is no denying that their hearts, although at enmity with God, sense a need for love and acceptance, which can be found in the very person they reject, God. Although there are many humanitarian organizations throughout the world, who, in many cases, are professionals in addressing the physical needs of the millions, the believer is the only one who understands the preciousness of human souls because he believes in the value that its Author has placed upon it. He is willing to travel to great lengths to snatch them from destruction. Without neglecting the physical needs of the people, we must primarily look for an open door to present the gospel since it is the only message that saves the soul from all corruption.

We must understand that the time to enter the harvest is now. However, one must humbly realize that an evangelist is merely one who plants a seed in people's hearts. It is God's Holy Spirit who opens people's eyes to see the malnourished state of their souls. Once the message of salvation finds good soil within someone's heart, then it will bloom into a precious plant of faith that will never perish, no matter what the world throws at it. Not only are we to apply temporal clothing, which is our good works unto the lost, but also robes of righteousness, in hopes of bringing the holy warmth of the gospel to their cold and naked souls, delivering them from the shame of their sinfulness. With all that said, will you not take up the call to serve alongside the Lord whose harvest is plentiful but the laborers few?

CHAPTER 12

BEHOLD, HE COMES

"So Christ, having been offered once to bear the sins of many, will appear a second time, not to deal with sin but to save those who are eagerly waiting for him."

Hebrews 9:28

A DESIRE FOR GREATER THINGS is ingrained in humanity. Many anticipate the next technological invention of man. Some wait on their work promotion, counting days to get ownership of a new home or motor vehicle, dreaming of the next getaway adventure, or imagining a retirement haven to spend the rest of their days on earth in luxurious ease. But I wonder how many desire the day of the One "coming with the clouds" (Rev. 1:7) "with ten thousands of his holy ones" (Jude 1:14) "to execute judgment on all and to convict all the ungodly of all their deeds of ungodliness that they have committed in such an ungodly way, and of all the harsh things that ungodly sinners have spoken against him" (Jude 1:15). And are Christians living in accordance to the promise that the Lord is coming "to save those who are eagerly waiting for him" (Heb. 9:28).

What would be your response if I posed the question, "How much of the Lord's presence do you desire daily?" If spending half an hour reading the Bible makes you anxiously look at the clock, how will you spend timeless days with the One Whose presence fills Heaven? The more of His presence you desire, the less of the world you admire. Sin becomes unattractive and holiness the heart's pursuit. These are the days of scoffers who say, "Where is the promise of His coming? For ever since the fathers fell asleep, all things are continuing as they were from the beginning of creation" (2 Peter 3:4). Not only were such people to be found in the apostle's days, but there are also still many whose unconcerned approaches to the Lord's coming and devoid of preparedness reflect this Scripture.

I remember being presented as a new believer by an evangelist with a very simple yet profound exhortation. The evangelist said, "If the Lord were coming tonight and you were the first one to know about it, what changes would you make in your life? How many souls would you evangelize, and how many doors would you knock on? With what great urgency would you shout out the message of the gospel? All this with only a few hours remaining until His return?" These straight-to-the-point questions would leave me perplexed for a long time with their intense implications for my spiritual readiness and the souls of the unconverted.

I have been a part of many Christian circles throughout my time in the United States. Many were Bible studies, where most seemed to draw more excitement from the upcoming football games, television shows, movies, and latest fashion trends, rather than from the second coming of the Lord Jesus Christ for His bride. The joy and boasting of this singular event should far surpass any momentary events in life, or so I thought. The message that elevated the early church in its call to holiness and obedience has been plastered over with a pitiable invitation to relaxation and separation from the reality of the soon-coming King. After all, it should not be surprising because the so-called preachers of our generation would much rather offend God over their donors, for such a call to get one's household in order and live lives worthy of the gospel demands swift obedience, which to an unbelieving heart is foreign and too costly. Such preaching would empty almost the entire congregation, leaving the preacher bankrupt and out of business. If the Lord is coming soon, there remains no time to waste; instead, let every fleeting second be given over to the service of His Majesty in Heaven.

"Who then is the faithful and wise servant, whom his master has set over his household, to give them their food at the proper time? Blessed is that servant whom his master will find so doing when he comes. Truly, I say to you, he will set him over all his possessions. But if that wicked servant says to himself, 'My master is delayed,' and begins to beat his fellow servants and eats and drinks with drunkards, the master of that servant will come on a day when he does not expect him and at an hour he does not know and will cut him in pieces and put him with the hypocrites. In that place there will be weeping and gnashing of teeth" (Matt. 24:45-51).

Faithful and wise is he who prepares his soul through word-filled obedience and those of fellow servants as he waits upon the Master and is met with His good pleasure over his steadfast perseverance in serving. The latter's wickedness lies in not believing the Master's word, "Therefore you also must be ready, for the Son of Man is coming at an hour you do not expect." (Matt. 24:44) Contrary to the Master's word, this servant excuses himself the responsibility of feeding those under his care with the Word. Instead, he indulges in selfish pleasure, all the while treating the fellow servants with contempt and great neglect; the servant is met with the Master's displeasure at His return. The rebellion that grew in the mind motivated the heart to abandon its assigned duty, thus producing a lifestyle that the Lord deemed worthy of Hell. All of which originated through deviating from the Lord's command of readiness for His return. The difference between the two servants is that one faithfully abided in his post, whereas the other forsook it for sin.

Why has the Lord tarried for over two thousand years? The answer is that He is patient toward mankind, not wishing that any should perish but that all should reach repentance (2 Peter 3:9). The time of waiting is for days of gathering. We cannot afford to waste the days of mercy since the day of vengeance is right around the corner. Mercy befriends the penitent and wrath the impenitent; so then, rise, oh Christian, and blow the trump of the eternal gospel until your voice gives out, the heart stops beating, and the soul enters rest. For if we remain quiet on the day of mercy, we will find ourselves blushing with shame on the day of wrath. When mindful of the Lord's soon return, one cannot continue in their backslidden state of indifferent living. Instead, their soul would be filled with the reality of standing before the One whose eyes are too pure to look upon evil and cannot tolerate wrongdoing. Having unforgiven sins presented before such a One would make your soul sprint to His mercy rather than continuing in a lifestyle contrary to His calling to stand apart from the wicked world.

The Lord is a Treasure to those who do all His work with pleasure. And remind you, He is no Christian who values earthly possessions over the person of Christ. One of the modern-day tragedies is that many in the church have lost sight of the imminent return of the Rider on the white horse, Who, accompanied by innumerable hosts of Heaven, is coming to rule and reign forever. Many may acknowledge this event doctrinally but their actions condemn them. It is the reason for the spiritually apathetic lifestyles of the masses who live as though the King were never coming back, proving their disloyalty to Him by choosing earth's fleeting happiness over Heaven's incomprehensible joy.

"Come quickly," says the Bride to her Bridegroom, and the deeper the love of the Bride, the more intense the desire to be with Him. It is the world she desires to bid goodbye, not only to escape its sinful corruptions as much as to behold the One Whom she was made for. The Bridegroom's blood was shed for her so she could clothe herself with the whitest and purest wedding garment imaginable. She is placed upon the most honorable wedding feast table and, above all, to gaze and marvel at a love so endearing which has engraved her name upon the Bridegroom's heart. The Bridegroom wants to draw the Bride to Himself with the cords of His love and by bestowing a single eye of adoration to the revelation of the fullness of His character, beckoning her to fly and nest herself in the comfort of His bosom.

Whether people believe it or not, the Lord is coming back for a ready bride who has purified herself by waiting upon her beloved's promises. He is undoubtedly not returning for a prostitute who claims the rights of a bride but defiles her wedding garments by pledging loyalty to the world's influence. The Bridegroom died to make His Bride pure and rose from the dead to keep her pure. Tell me, when was the last time you worshipped with tears of gratitude, knowing who you were formerly and who Christ has made you be forevermore?

"You also, be patient. Establish your hearts, for the coming of the Lord is at hand" (James 5:8). "Let your reasonableness be known to everyone. The Lord is at hand" (Phil. 4:5). These words were penned down two thousand years ago; and if that generation felt that they were close to the coming of the Lord, oh, how much closer is the present God-hating generation to the second coming? The former calls for patience and the latter gentleness, which many have forsaken. This has resulted in a swift departure from simple and steadfast trust and driven many into intellectual and worldly hurdles, which has converted many into scoffers and away from the faith they once confessed. After all, sin's fleeting pleasure and its glamorized marketing have bewitched many pew dwellers through unconverted preaching that bids the soul to desire things of lesser value while covering the seeking eye with a veil of entertainment. It leaves them with a false sense of peace and security which the Lord, at His coming, will expose the house founded on sand for what it really is, accursed assurance. Whether you are taken away from this life through death or left alive until His second coming, it should not hold any bearing on your readiness to meet the Lord.

"Heavens and earth that now exist are stored up for fire, being kept until the day of judgment and destruction of the ungodly" (2 Peter 3:7). "Since all these things are thus to be dissolved, what sort of people ought you to be in lives of holiness and godliness, waiting for and hastening the coming of the day of God, because of which the heavens will be set on fire and dissolved, and the heavenly bodies will melt as they burn" (2 Peter 3:11-12). We are to live holy and godly lives as we eagerly await the Lord's return; but tragically, we have dismissed such a calling as living in fanaticism and legalism. Nevertheless, holiness and godliness, when lived out, keep the soul in great awareness and anticipation of the Bridegroom's return.

What part of His imminent return are we not grasping? For example, the Lord says, "'Behold, I am coming like a thief! Blessed is the one who stays awake, keeping his garments on, that he may not go about naked and be seen exposed'" (Rev. 16:15). I believe prayer quickens the slumbering soul and keeps it awake. In addition, the garments are the "work of faith and labor of love and steadfastness of hope" (1 Thess. 1:3). At the same time, the nakedness applies to those unclothed with the former's fruit, leaving them in for a dreadful awakening at the Lord's returns.

One of the most painful grievances to the Lord is a supposed saint living in the lost world like an unsaved heathen. If an unbelieving eye can spot your lifestyle to be no different than theirs, you had better put on sackcloth and ashes and not rest until the Lord assures your sonship and makes you an instrument of His praise. Lack of urgency in this area of the Lord's return shows your lack of concern for His Word and, I dare say, your faith in His Word. "Let us eat and drink, for tomorrow we die," says the callous soul who trades the comfort of Heaven for earth's misery, whereas the mindful look above for their resting place: "But my eyes are toward you, O GOD, my Lord; in you I seek refuge; leave me not defenseless" (Psalm 141:8).

Every eye will behold the King Who appears in the clouds, while sinners will melt away with terror at the sheer sight. The Bride clothed in His robes of perfect righteousness will be overcome with holy reverence mingled with inexpressible joy. It will be an incredible sight for the redeemed but a horror for the unredeemed. The scoffing hearts of those uninspired by the Word of God will be inspired by shame to look away from the blinding appearance of His perfect, glorious presence. This will occur as the Bible says, "When he comes on that day to be glorified in his saints, and to be marveled at among all who have believed" (2 Thess. 1:10). Therefore, "Let the evildoer still do evil, and the filthy still be filthy, and the righteous still do right, and the holy still be holy. Behold, I am coming soon, bringing my recompense with me, to repay each one for what he has done. I am the Alpha and the Omega, the first and the last, the beginning and the end" (Rev. 22:11-13). "He who testifies to these things says, "Surely I am coming soon." Amen. Come, Lord Jesus" (Rev. 22:20).

CHAPTER 13

MEN NEEDED FOR TODAY

"The prophets prophesy falsely, and the priests rule at their direction;
my people love to have it so, but what will you do when the end comes."

Jeremiah 5:31

IN THIS CURRENT FAMINE-STRICKEN WORLD for the Word of God, we have quite a lot of self-proclaimed prophets scattered throughout the land. They strut around with their heads held high in pride, spreading their selfish agenda to enlarge their pockets. Unlike the prophets of old, these men are famous. You can be sure that a prophet is unpopular because the message he brings gets backlash from the majority. The message that this kind of prophet delivers is like nails driven through the backslidden conscience by the hammer of God's Word, and it demands a response. This prophet gets the message from the Throne room of God and delivers it without altering it. His message stands out due to its urgent nature, as it should be because the hour of the Lord's return is imminent.

Through the lens of deception, the sleepy church sings, "peace and security," whereas the prophet sees every circumstance through the eyes of God and warns everyone of the impending disaster that the blind are headed into. Loyalty to God marks his genuineness, and friendship with the world is quickly shunned. Such men are always rare; and one cannot find them out in the open because they are hidden by God Himself, only to be revealed at God's final call to mercy before He brings judgment. A prophet's fear is overcome by the assurance of God's presence. Thus, he can preach the Word at any cost, even in the face of unwillingness, which quickly melts away by the fire of the Word, at which point he cannot help but feel the burning of the implanted word of God bidding him to speak.

Therefore, his burden is only lifted after the kindled Word of God is proclaimed. What renders a prophet dangerous is not his physical appearance but his level of intimacy with God. This kind of intimate bond brings God's resources to his disposal, turning many nations and peoples toward God's mercy and, at times, toward judgment. Reconciliation of the sinner to God is what moves a prophet's heart, and he will travel to great lengths to see its fruition. Such faithful service to the Lord makes him the instant target of a sin-embracing and God-rejecting crowd whose unholy hearts cannot endure the holy words of God. Despite the tear-filled pleadings that the prophet pours out over those whom he desires saved, they repay the good with evil and persecute him, and in some cases, even unto death.

While there are many prophets we read about in the Bible, the ministries of Elijah and John the Baptist stand out prominently. When the nation of Israel had become corrupt beyond recognition, God deployed a man, Elijah, as a rod of reproof for the nation, starting with the royals, all the way down to its subjects. The nation that Elijah was to speak to had, along with its king, betrayed God to serve instead a blood-thirsty deity named Baal. When King Ahab took the throne, the land was even more polluted as idolatry ran rampant in the people's hearts. After four hundred years of moral and spiritual decline and no word from the Lord, God finally sent a prophet named John the Baptist as a trumpeter of repentance to prepare the people's hearts for the coming Messiah's indwelling. John the Baptist came in the spirit of Elijah, dressed like Elijah, and in the message of Elijah to confront the nation of its sins and bring its faithless inhabitants back to the faithfulness of God.

These men were both sent to the lost nation of Israel when true religion was reaching its end. Although strictly observed, the law was gravely abused and forsaken in reality. Idolatry and greed had swallowed up the entire nation of Israel. While God could have sent His mighty archangels to chasten them, He instead sent out two prophets to speak to the people of Israel during these crucial hours in history. Finally, when God was fed up with a corrupt religious system, He raised John the Baptist from within and clothed him in the wilderness with true godliness. John the Baptist's zeal and love for God and His people greatly upset the spiritually bankrupt Pharisaic system.

"No! John! You are the son of a priest! How can you put off priestly garments and be clothed with the hair of an unholy camel? Would you feast upon insects and not the wonderful and fatty meat portion of the priests? Your father's reputation as a priest will be tarnished. And think sensibly! Is wilderness a place for a priest? Is it a place of order like the synagogues?" Such questions and reasonings were presented to John, I am sure. Unwilling to disobey his heavenly calling, he never looked back, of which I am all the more convinced.

And just as it was in Elijah's days, I am sure it is now that God has the seven thousand who have not and will not bow their knees to lukewarm Christianity. The God Who answers by fire is still the God Who answers His people through the fire of His Word, but the question is are you seeking Him? The burning bush still bids many to turn aside from life's distractions and encounter the awesome sight of God's presence. Are you willing to heed the call of God amidst the chaos of a busy life full of distractions? The prophets of Baal cannot prosper when Elijah-like men call the lukewarm Church to repentance. Nor can the Herods of our day remain comfortable in their immoral lifestyle when John the Baptist-like men lift the trump of warning.

A prophet exists to make God known and himself unknown. Humility clothes a prophet; and if we were to hear his heartbeat, it would echo with such words: "He must increase, but I must decrease" (John 3:30). They weep in secret for the eyes that are dry; they fast in secret for those whose appetite is filled with ungodly craving. They accept rejection and many cold shoulders to make the rejected welcome into the loving arms of God; and when sleep comes upon men, intercession clothes the prophet to awaken the sleepy ones. The so-called prophets of our day are inspired at giving personal opinions but uninspired when it comes to proclaiming the word of the Lord. Prophets are appointed by God and not chosen by men. They are called by God, not by their feelings.

They pledge their lives to God's Word before securing God's Word to the sinner's life. Their generation receives them with many blows, while the next generation welcomes them with a hearty salute. They are educated in the school of consecration and solitude, where the Spirit operates upon the heart, replacing the remnants of sinfulness with the cleansing coals from the burning altar, as it happened with Isaiah. After having the eyes of the heart opened to the holy nature of God and purified, he is then sent to the people with a burning message that urges the soul to declare God's words to the masses. A prophet's message often contains news of ongoing crises and future events, and no amount of water is strong enough to put out the flame of the Word. Nor will their eyes submit to sleep until their entire message is delivered. The revelation of God's broken heart breaks the prophet's heart, and his tears represent God's grievances over the people's sinfulness. "My eyes shed streams of tears," exclaims a prophet, "because people do not keep your law" (Psalm 119:136).

One crucial thing that one needs to understand is that prophets are made by God alone. You cannot attend seminary to obtain a degree that gives you the honor of learning how to become a prophet by intellectual means. One surely cannot attempt to buy it in exchange for earthly perishables. It is a calling that is incorruptible and beyond human reach. Many judge such men as being harsh, void of mercy, and with a gloomy perspective in life, not realizing that their weeping before God for the sins of their accusers allows them to breathe and enjoy the air of God's mercy. They ignorantly despise the instrument who, with the power of their prayers, hold back the wrath of the Almighty from obliterating the sons of disobedience.

The mercy of God is revealed in the prophet's pleading; and at the same time, the wrath of God is revealed when men suppress the voice of mercy. When a church lingers between serving God or the world, men like Elijah are brought on the scene with a correctional rod of God's equipping, at whose proclamation an answer is demanded. There is neither dancing around with words nor apologies for their passionate love toward God, which results in flipping idolatrous tables in people's hearts. His simple words filled with jealousy for God's name aim the piercing sword of the Spirit with great accuracy toward the direction of that which "is deceitful above all things and desperately sick" (Jer. 17:9)—the heart.

Would you be okay if God sent some Elijah-like prophets to confront the priests of the New Covenant who have committed many sins on account of their Jezebel-like, seductive preaching, normalizing their adulterous relationship with the world and giving approval for those who would pursue it? I believe many evangelical Christians would react like the Pharisees and Sadducees, who roared in anger against the preaching of repentance and holiness. Were John the Baptist to appear on the scene, it would rock the world of many so-called Christians caught up in the stagnant waters of a lukewarm lifestyle. Such men like John the Baptist and Elijah are God's handcrafted arrows, who are in the making as we speak, and being sharpened in the secrecy of the prayer closet. They are currently being baptized with the brokenness and zeal for God's glory and on the verge of being shot by the skillful archer from the armory of God's right hand, aimed at the hearts of many. The execution of the arrow results in mercy for the penitent and judgment for the wicked. Their singleness of eye for God's glory, mingled with a simplistic lifestyle that permeates the fragrance of godliness, will be honored by God as instruments that awaken and prepare the people for the second coming of the Lord Jesus Christ with all His saints.

"For the Lord GOD does nothing without revealing his secret to his servants the prophets" (Amos 3:7). So then, brethren, we had better heed the words of such men who are filled with the Spirit of truth. We do not need more preachers possessed with intellectual pride to strut from the pulpit. These are people good with words but having not an ounce of intimacy with God. A prophet knows not how to flatter nor practice arrogance. He is the voice that the Church of Jesus Christ needs for the tribulation that she is headed into. And yet, "'A prophet is not without honor, except in his hometown and among his relatives and in his own household'" (Mark 6:4). Oftentimes, the people acquainted with a prophet will be the first ones to declare him a lunatic, for isn't this the plumber, farmer, mechanic, janitor, cook, or even the carpenter that lives down the street? Aren't his family attending the same church as the rest of us? So they take offense at him.

I am sure everybody was just fine with the Carpenter from Nazareth until the sharp, two-edged sword of God's Word issued from His lips, upsetting many unconverted hearts. A prophet cannot mind his own business because his being is consumed with God's interests. He is moved, as God is. Upon seeing the idolatrous feast of the Israelites as he came down from Mount Sinai, Moses threw the two tablets of commandments onto the ground in holy anger, breaking them into pieces. Moses felt angry (Exod. 32:19) because God was angry (Exod. 32:10). Forty days and nights of beholding God Almighty left Moses fused to God, implanting God's Divine emotions into his mortal human heart.

Making the Lord smile is the joy of the prophet and the grievances of the Lord become the burden of the prophet. While many would like to claim the mantle of Moses' authority, Elijah's power, and John the Baptist's preaching, how many are willing to be clothed in the sackcloth of their rejection, persecution, and poverty? The false prophets are famous because "they speak visions of their own minds, not from the mouth of the LORD. They say continually to those who despise the word of the LORD, 'It shall be well with you'; and to everyone who stubbornly follows his own heart, they say, 'No disaster shall come upon you'" (Jer. 23:16-17). Such men are nothing new and were even praised during Jeremiah's day. These wicked men had infiltrated places of great influence, even as counselors to kings.

"An appalling and horrible thing has happened in the land: the prophets prophesy falsely, and the priests rule at their direction; my people love to have it so, but what will you do when the end comes" (Jer. 5:30-31). But are the preachers and prophets the only ones to invite judgment upon themselves, or are the hearers just as much involved in their iniquities? God's indictment is not only with those who tickle ears but also those who love to have theirs tickled, "who say to the seers, 'Do not see,' and to the prophets, 'Do not prophesy to us what is right; speak to us smooth things, prophesy illusions, leave the way, turn aside from the path, let us hear no more about the Holy One of Israel'" (Isa. 30:10-11). Sadly, we face the same crisis today as people are given what they want to hear rather than what the Lord needs them to hear. This cycle starts from God's house and goes as far up the social ladder as to reach even the doors of the White House. The Holy One will not bear with it much longer and will soon unmask their lying deception and expose the corrupt messengers of Satan through the Jeremiahs of the coming days.

Do not worry, oh preserved few and faithful, the prophets of the world, flesh, and the devil with all their trickery will not sway your pure devotion from the One Who fills the altar of your heart with the flames of His abounding love and enduring faithfulness. Like the psalmist, you can confidently proclaim that "God in his steadfast love will meet me; God will let me look in triumph on my enemies" (Psalm 59:10); and since your heart has not gone after what your eye has seen, God will satisfy your eyes with contentment and fill your heart with purity. The voice of the false prophets may plague the land through radio, television, conferences, educational systems, workplaces, and even the pulpit. Take heart and be rest assured that the Shepherd's voice will continue to call those with ears to hear the words of eternal life through the often-rejected, culturally removed, and greatly scorned prophets before the great and terrible day of the Lord. So then, pray always and listen closely to catch every word that He gives you through holy men who are filled with the Holy Spirit.

"Therefore, my beloved brothers, be steadfast, immovable, always abounding in the work of the Lord, knowing that in the Lord your labor is not in vain" (1 Cor. 15:58). "Would that all the LORD's people were prophets, and that the LORD would put his Spirit on them" (Num. 11:29).

CHAPTER 14

DISTRACTED CHURCH IN A PERISHING WORLD

"For my people have committed two evils: they have forsaken me,
the fountain of living waters, and hewed out cisterns for themselves,
broken cisterns that can hold no water."

Jeremiah 2:13

AMID FIERY TRIALS, THE EARLY church stood unmoved and was marked with contentment. Whereas the freedom of our day has crippled the Church, leaving it chasing after incessant entertainment. I would run out of time on this earth if I were to speak of all the men and women I have encountered, who, in their early years, served the Lord with remarkable zeal but then, sadly, had their flame diminish over the years as the desire to be amused by the television outgrew their joy to serve the Lord and behold His glory. I have been in the United States for quite some time now and have become acquainted with most of its church culture and traditions. There is one thing that continues to baffle me is our love for sports.

My jaw dropped when I first read of preachers dismissing the pew early for the sake of sports. Some would attend the early morning service to not miss a game in the late afternoon. Being raised in a pagan household, I thought I had been exposed to the epitome of idolatry until witnessing these events in the United States. I believe that God has pronounced Ichabod over such congregations; and astoundingly, many do not even know it. After having visited many churches and spoken to countless congregants, I have noticed that there seems to be more excitement over the next football or baseball game than there is about winning souls for the glory of Jesus Christ.

Millions of eyes are transfixed upon the scoreboards of sports games. At the same time, the devil covers their eyes, blinding them to the things of eternity. While possessing a wealth of knowledge regarding the rules and player statistics of various sports, many at the same time are bankrupt in their understanding of the words of eternal life. They will gladly submit themselves to an hour and a half of cheering. In contrast, an hour of worship is reluctantly agreed upon with coldness. If such fleeting happiness were yielded for God's glory in the service of evangelism, God's power would have swept many sinners into the Kingdom.

"I will not set before my eyes anything that is worthless. I hate the work of those who fall away; it shall not cling to me" (Psalm 101:3). We cannot behold the fullness of the presence of God if we set our eyes before that which is worthless. For example, I remember attending a dinner meeting at a deacon's house, whose daughter was there and happened to be a Sunday school assistant at a local church. While discussing the need for purity in the Church, the daughter interjected with a shocking statement regarding her belief about sexual relationships.

"There is nothing wrong with a man and a woman loving each other unto fornication. As a matter of fact, I recently watched a romantic movie about this very topic," she stated.

I was left utterly speechless and gasping for my next breath.

To compound my shock, the deacon then supported her claim rather than rebuke his daughter as he sat there nodding his head with a smile on his face. Having lost my appetite and being choked up for words, I left the house overcome with grief. I have been a part of such instances; and throughout the years, I have noticed that such claims are not believed or lived out overnight but through a gradual deviation from God's Word.

The blessed Spirit is grieved every time we neglect the cause of the Lord Jesus Christ. To put it clearly and simply, you must choose to serve God wholeheartedly; or you cannot serve Him at all. The command to "come follow Me" is not the path of your leading. Instead, it is God's call for you to set foot on the narrow road to salvation. Once you start your walk on the narrow road, you must continue looking upward for guidance. The King will not enlist an earth-bound man who gets himself entangled by the amusements of this life in the heavenly quest of recruiting soldiers for the cross. "No soldier gets entangled in civilian pursuits, since his aim is to please the one who enlisted him" (2 Tim. 2:4). This lesson is one that our generation of church attendees would do well to heed.

We are all marching toward the valley of decision, where we must choose between God and our idols. What appeared spiritual for decades is getting ready to be exposed as nothing but a reliance on the frailty of human strength. How can we cross over the Red Sea while the idols of Egypt are among us? And how can we inherit the promises of God while worshipping the gods of Canaan? The stories of Abraham, Moses, David, Paul, and other biblical figures reveal that, as they aged, they increasingly fixed their gaze upon God. In contrast, many elders in our churches seem fixated on television, thus falling prey to man's vision.

Television is not inherently dangerous; but it becomes your idol when you passionately defend it, and many people fall into this trap. No wonder human vision captivates the heart with excitement, while the passion to live for Almighty God leaves the entertained heart feeling bored. "The children have lost their way and become twice or thrice as ungodly than the heathens," says the parent who, instead of groaning for their child's salvation, spent countless hours weeping and romanticizing over God-hating television shows. They closely monitored the scoreboard of a sports game while turning a blind eye to their souls' needs and relinquished their responsibility to a government institution instead of raising them with sacrificial love. Simply put, they have failed their children who needed a man or a woman to imitate in the ways of godliness and good conduct.

I would instantly befriend angry voices and the scorn of many churchgoers should I bring up in conversation the subject of laying aside idols, especially the television. Why will you not set apart those hours of vain television shows, Netflix, and other platforms for time spent in the Word of God, prayer, and fasting? Besides, 99.9 percent of what is seen on television is an insult to a Holy God. Tell me then, would the Spirit of God who is in you allow you to behold sexual immorality, slander, gossip, witchcraft, drunkenness, thievery, and other unmentionable sins without striking the soul with any level of grievances?

If you should say yes, then you are far from Him, whose eyes are too pure to look upon sin. It would be fair to say that you have an unconverted heart if the sorrow of the Holy Spirit is not realized or felt in your inner person. We do not even realize the injury we bring upon our souls when we partake in the very thing the Spirit is delivering us from. Your stagnant sanctification is not due to God's timing but rather your abuse of grace. Our freedom was given to us for love-filled service and not selfish indulgence; therefore, "do not use your freedom as an opportunity for the flesh, but through love serve one another" (Gal. 5:13). "Live as people who are free, not using your freedom as a cover-up for evil, but living as servants of God" (1 Peter 2:16). So what can one do to crucify worldly distractions and instead pursue the presence of God?

Two things that can be done to devote time and effort to God are fasting and prayer. And yet, both of these things are often only grudgingly done. For instance, fasting has become a foreign term to many in the Church, and prayer is something that is merely said without reverence or fervor. Many prayers never reach the throne room because the issuing hearts cherish iniquity. In fact, prayers that flow through the hearts of those who despise the Word of God are considered an abomination to Him (Psalm 66:18; Prov. 28:9), who through His Word is working in us (1 Thess. 2:13).

The Lord's message for the Church has always been about holiness, and the ones to take up the call are the remnants who have tasted and seen the Lord's goodness (Psalm 34:8), "who loves purity of heart, and whose speech is gracious"; therefore, they "will have the King as his friend" (Prov. 22:11). Just this past Sunday, I am sure that many idolatrous men and women walked down the altar for a quick prayer and consolation; and unchanged, they walked out of the doors of the Church and entered right back into a sinful lifestyle. They come to the altar because they know that what they are doing is not right, but the preacher says otherwise. Rather than letting the Spirit burn the idols through conviction and cleansing, they are made to repeat a prayer and an assured victory while the idols in their hearts live on.

There are important things to remember as shallow, half-measured calls to salvation continue to be spoken from the pulpit. For example, take how Almighty God was even fed up with the state of His people during Jeremiah's days when the Lord says, "The priests did not say, 'Where is the LORD?' Those who handle the law did not know me; the shepherds transgressed against me; the prophets prophesied by Baal and went after things that do not profit" (Jer. 2:8). And when God is sickened by what is taking place inside the Church, to the point of vomiting in utter disgust, He sent a prophet to declare these words:

> Behold, you trust in deceptive words to no avail. Will you steal, murder, commit adultery, swear falsely, make offerings to Baal, and go after other gods that you have not known, and then come and stand before me in this house, which is called by my name, and say, "We are delivered!"—only to go on doing all these abominations? Has this house, which is called by my name, become a den of robbers in your eyes? Behold, I myself have seen it, declares the LORD (Jer. 7:8-11).

Sadly, I am sure many will simply shrug their shoulders and push away these warnings as irrelevant because the present-day Baal has blinded the minds of the worshippers of entertainment and pleasure, keeping them in a state of indifference toward God's presence. These people are profaning the sanctuary through an unbroken, unaware heart that does not sense the Spirit's holy presence. With that being said, we cannot afford to abandon our post, slumber on watch duty, or fall asleep while reading God's Word. The world is speeding its way to Hell with nobody sounding the alarm for the millions walking in the broad path of destruction. There is no time for distraction during these critical hours. I urge you to put off all the unnecessary weight of indulgence and the sin of empty justification, which only carry us away from God's lovely presence and bury us in hopeless wandering. But let us finish the course set before us as we "put on the Lord Jesus Christ, and make no provision for the flesh, to gratify its desires" (Rom. 13:14).

If we profess Heaven to be our home, then why are we heaping possessions on earth? We bow our heads to God on Sundays with a game of pretentious seeking and yield our members as an instrument for sin's bidding for the remainder of the week. With a testimony as marred and embarrassing as this, we cannot win a single soul, let alone win the world to Christ. I know of many people who were running the race, climbing the plateau of holiness, and excelling beyond people their age when suddenly, their eye drifted away from the Author of life and uncrucified temptation made their hearts befriend and live for the fleeting pleasures of America. Worldly pleasures stopped them from running and reversing the course toward the slavish schemes of the former life after being set free from it.

Brethren! Did Christ die to free us so that we could continue to live for ourselves? Do you not realize that Jesus "died for all, that those who live might no longer live for themselves but for him who for their sake died and was raised" (2 Cor. 5:15). He died to make us His so that we could make Him ours. I have personally met Christians who are awakened to the global warming crisis but unconcerned about the millions perishing in heathendom.

In this generation of churches, most of these believers are entirely unprepared to tackle the coming global crisis of overwhelming and unrestrained iniquity, which the devil is getting ready to vomit out upon the world. In doing so, the devil will focus on the faithful remnant, like a master assassin peering through a rifle's scope. The only ones to endure the coming flood of deadly deception will be the Christians who courageously persevered and clung to their precious faith through the famines, plagues, and poverty of the end times.

> A son honors his father, and a servant his master. If then I am a father, where is my honor? And if I am a master, where is my fear? says the LORD of hosts to you, O priests, who despise my name. But you say, "How have we despised your name?" By offering polluted food upon my altar. But you say, "How have we polluted you?" By saying that the LORD's table may be despised. When you offer blind animals in sacrifice, is that not evil? And when you offer those that are lame or sick, is that not evil? Present that to your governor; will he accept you or show you favor? says the LORD of hosts (Mal. 1:6-8).

Oh, preachers and ministers of the Word, when was the last time you examined your offering before presenting it to God? God's name is despised when you offer handicapped sacrifices, whether done by yourselves or by those who offer half-hearted devotion. In pretense, these people display reverence while storing up iniquity within. They outwardly pray for purity and yet inwardly burn with immoral passions and use Christ's name and compassion as a cloak to cover up the abuses of His precious graces and promote man-centered ideologies.

Is this not evil? Present such an attitude to your supervisors and see how long you last in the workforce. God says, "Oh, that there were one among you who would shut the doors, that you might not kindle fire on my altar in vain! I have no pleasure in you, says the LORD of hosts, and I will not accept an offering from your hand" (Mal. 1:10). God will not accept an offering of absolute disregard to His holiness. Therefore, it is better not to sacrifice anything at all than to present unholy lives at the altar, no matter the spiritual appearance of the offering or its quantity. For it is not the material that God seeks in worship as much as you offering "your bodies as a living sacrifice, holy and acceptable to God" (Rom. 12:1). When the latter is presented in that manner, the former will be accepted as well.

Alas! This generation wants God without obedience and obedience without sacrifice and sacrifice of their own choosing, which has to fit into their schedule. After all, we get to pick how and when to serve God. Do we, as Christians in America, not have the freedom and rights to enjoy the fruit of our hard-earned money for selfish pleasure? The answer is yes, if you are an American Christian in the American economy, but absolutely not if you are a Heavenly Christian on Christ's economy. Do not treasure anything in life that cannot be taken in death; for only the works of faith, the labor of love, and steadfastness of hope shall enter through the gates of Heaven by which the King of glory Himself entered. The devil laughs at our so-called rational questions, such as, "If it is not sin, or stated as such, why not partake in it?" That being said, I believe that is one of the questions that the Dragon uses to lure the target into the bait of temptation and distraction. The deceiver's tactics are to draw away many gullible souls to what appears as a non-sinful thought, activity, or even lifestyle. After catching the prey with the cleverly devised snare of passivity, the devil, although not able to possess a Christian, will exercise blinding influence by keeping the Christian fast asleep to the effectiveness of his ransomed soul and wide awake to the things that appeal to the flesh.

Distraction, if not arrested, becomes steps that blindly lead one to sin without warning. Beware, even the godliest of men can fall into its trap. Bring all your distractions to the foot of the cross and crucify them so you will be free from its unnecessary weight and run the race as a runner to obtain the prize of an imperishable wreath, which is how you ought to run. Whoever sacrifices reluctantly does not yet understand the priceless worth of the one to whom he renders the offering. If "God loves a cheerful giver" (2 Cor. 9:7), let us give cheerfully, lest our giving be in vain.

"Let us test and examine our ways, and return to the Lord" (Lam. 3:40)! If your eyes are currently wandering, torn between serving the Lord or self, make a decisive choice today. Choose whether to serve the god of the American Dream or the god of entertainment, sports, and pleasure. But as for the blood-bought servants of the Lord Jesus Christ, we will serve the Lamb Who has triumphed over the grave and overcome the world. With all that being said, Brethren, I implore you to crucify the short-lived ecstasies derived from your earthly treasures and instead consider these words: "Come, everyone who thirsts, come to the waters; and he who has no money, come, buy and eat! Come, buy wine and milk without money and without price. Why do you spend your money for that which is not bread, and your labor for that which does not satisfy? Listen diligently to me, and eat what is good, and delight yourselves in rich food (Isa. 55:1-2).

CHAPTER 15

MINISTRY OF BEHOLDING

"Moses said, 'Please show me your glory."

Exodus 33:18

LIKE MARY, OUR GENERATION OF Christians would be more effective in their ministry if they sat by the Lord's feet, beholding His glorious presence in speechless adoration. However, they are like Martha, who allowed serving to get in the way of surveying. Many of God's weary servants, in the name of ministry, have labored much for the service of the cross but brought great injury upon their souls by replacing the Master's presence with their performance. The strength of a Christian is not obtained through the work of the Lord but rather by quieting the soul in the Lord's presence. As a result, the child of God is refreshed and empowered for the service to which he is called.

A Christian is called to behold the Lord if he desires to fulfill his ministry effectively. Even if a Christian possessed great knowledge on how to harvest souls but did not lean unto the Lord of the harvest for guidance, he would blunt the blade of the sickle and reap nothing. In vain, he would swing without any effect on the crops. How should the work of the Lord proceed further when the Lord of the work is nowhere to be found? Time and time again, we are told to wait upon the Lord. But what sort of waiting is this?

It is a patient waiting on God that takes us into the holy of holies to behold His lovely face; and as a result, our strength is renewed and vision purified. Waiting on God means patiently beholding Him. Power and perseverance come from beholding the Lord, whether in secret or with fellow believers. I have spoken to former and current missionaries from different countries, most of whom express more love for their work than the God who employed them. Even the most spiritual duties—such as evangelism, helping the poor, feeding the orphans, taking care of widows, and practicing hospitality—can be nullified when the eye is raised too high and the heart is pumping with too much pride in oneself. One should not look solely at the fruit of one's ministries rather than bowing in gratitude to the One "from whom the whole body, joined and held together by every joint with which it is equipped, when each part is working properly, makes the body grow so that it builds itself up in love" (Eph. 4:16).

We can envision lofty things, labor with all our strength, and sometimes convince ourselves of God's approval of our work. The work, however, if driven by presumption instead of its Author, may appear convincing but lifeless at the core. God's work without His presence can be likened to a hired cook who undertakes the duty of the Master chef without his recipe. How can we not let the cart in front of the horse? The answer is "looking to Jesus, the founder and perfecter of our faith" (Heb. 12:2) and to be still and know that God is Who He says He is. We need to meditate on the awesomeness of God's character, the same revelation of which made Moses instantly bow in worship (Exod. 34:6-8).

Worship at its highest is basking in the revelation of God's character with speechless awe. When was the last time you fell and bowed in worship because the Lord descended upon the soul, filling it with an unutterable and surpassing revelation of who He is? Like Moses, Joshua was another fascinating man of God who was committed to God. Concerning this man, the Bible says, "When Moses turned again into the camp, his assistant Joshua the son of Nun, a young man, would not depart from the tent" (Exod. 33:11). This tent that Joshua refused to depart from was where God would manifest His power. Thus, Joshua wanted to be around constantly so he would not miss a thing when God gave a glimpse of His glory from within the tent. What Joshua had was a deep, reverent love for God and a hunger to behold Him constantly.

For a Christian, the hunger to behold the presence must surpass that of any work, no matter its spiritual stature. There are no shortcuts to gain this nature of hunger for God's glory. The only way it can be obtained is through beholding the presence. The more you behold His presence, the more you desire it. The truly spiritual man desires God for Who God is and, in the same way, the Spirit of God before he desires the gifts of the Spirit. Panting after God can only be issued from the soul that wants God for Who He is. If your chief motivation to desire after God does not spring from that revelation, then you had better, through repentance, seek the inexpressible joy of His presence until it is bestowed.

The writer of the Book of Psalms expresses his joyous contentment in the Shepherd's leading and preserving the sheep when he says, "The LORD is my Shepherd; I shall not want" (Psalm 23:1). It sums up the Christian who is satisfied by the Lord's presence, not wanting anything less or more. But if hunger comes from beholding, where does the hunger to behold come from? The simple answer is to ask God for it and, with faith, believe that you have received it. God will never reject a soul who desires the fullness of His presence, no matter how faithless you have been in the past; for repentance mingled with humility brings Divine mercy speedily to your aid.

I believe the glory of God is the presence of God, and we see this when Moses desperately asks to see the glory and receives it in the proclamation of God's awesome character (Exod. 33:18, 34:5-7). Whoever desires to enter the fullness of His presence must believe and meditate upon the glorious character of His person. Hence, brethren, tarry in the presence, which will make sweet the most bitter of work. Amen.

Our many failed attempts to reach the outside world with its clamorous demands can be attributed to our lack of beholding God in solitude. One hour spent in holy stillness before His presence is more fruitful than spending multiple hours in Christless ventures. Have we forgotten what happened when the faithless Israelites presumed to go to war against their enemies, thinking God would give them victory? They were met with a humiliating defeat. How about when the Israelites assumed that having the ark of the covenant in their possession was what brought them victory instead of obeying the One whose dwelling in it subdued their enemies (Num. 14:42-45; I Sam. 4:3-11)?

These presumptuous acts only led them to tragic defeats. We must have the presence of God go before us, and He will do so if we honor His work according to His ways. Rivers of ink have been drained, and innumerable pages have been printed about man's interpretation of God's work. These literary works invite failure because only God's vision brings the work of ministry to fruition.

The most enduring of God's laborers are those who find rest in His presence, allowing their character to be strengthened for the tasks ahead. Without this rest, the work risks incurring God's displeasure in testing times. Oh that we would be allowed to gaze upon the beauty of the fullness of His presence. Until then, may we stand confident with unwavering faith because this is the promise He has made to us: "I will see you again, and your hearts will rejoice, and no one will take your joy from you" (John 16:22). We "will see his face, and his name will be on their foreheads" (Rev. 22:4). If God Almighty has made known unto you the path of life or if He has brought you out from the kingdom of darkness into the kingdom of light, should your saved soul not be filled with indescribable anticipation to serve your Redeemer at any cost (Psalm 16:11)?

God is near to those who seek His presence continually but distant to those who surrender their lives sparingly. The secret counsel of the Lord is with those who love to spend time with Him in secrecy. As for the righteous, they behold God's face in righteousness; when they awake, they are satisfied with His likeness (Psalm 17:15). What reveals the level of a Christian's maturity is the way he or she reacts when confronted with their sins. Their sensitivity toward the things of God reflects their intimacy with Him all the more. For example, after he had sinned by not obeying the word of the Lord, Saul begged Samuel to uphold him in honor, despite his moral failures. The confrontation of King David's sin led him to walk in the repentant valley of humiliation at the expense of his reputation.

Saul highly esteemed the presence of God while the nation had reached the pinnacle of victory and prosperity, but he quickly turned faithless when hit with adversity. David, on the other hand, came to embrace the sweetness of the Presence through hardships and persecutions and dreaded the departure of God's Spirit from him after he had sinned. "I have sinned; yet honor me now" (I Sam. 15:30), said King Saul after failing to keep the charge of the Lord against the Amalekites. "Take not your Holy Spirit from me" (Psalm 51:11), said King David after committing murder and adultery. It is clear who loved the presence more than the prize and the giver more than the gift.

Saul desired an earthly kingdom, but David desired the King of Heaven. Great was the sin of King David, greater his repentance, and greater still the mercy of God toward a penitent David. King David was a man after God's heart because God had his heart and could freely lead, guide, and chasten David when needed. Every child of God should thus open their hearts to the Spirit's influence, which will then instill in them the most profound tenderness toward the things of God, birthing soul agony at the mere thought of grieving the presence of Love.

CHAPTER 16

WHAT IS THE SECRET?

"So that Christ may dwell in your hearts through faith."

Ephesians 3:17

HOW MANY TIMES HAVE WE read missionary biographies, raved about their mighty exploits for the Son of God, and asked ourselves, "What is the secret to their Christian life?" The simplest answer to this question is that they were "fully convinced that God was able to do what he had promised" (Rom. 4:21). We have what can rightly and sadly be called logical faith, which, if not in agreement with one's intellect, is quickly tossed away as unexplainable and, therefore, not worth believing. Science only allows the human mind to observe creation.

In contrast, the spiritual mind lets faith penetrate through the created object, leading the trail of its existence to the Almighty Himself. The names of our generation's top-ranked doctors, scientists, engineers, and architects have all made it to the front of our newspapers and magazines. They boast about their intellectual abilities to cure the incurable, solve the insolvable, discern the indiscernible, and plan the unplannable. These achievements are indeed honorable, but they are accepted with a heart of pride without ever mentioning the God in "whom are hidden all the treasures of wisdom and knowledge" (Col. 2:3), let alone giving Him the glory that He deserves.

In contrast, we have the great apostle Paul, who likened his intellectual zeal to a pile of trash because he had found the surpassing worth of knowing Christ to be infinitely more valuable (Phil. 3:8). Concerning this comparison of earthly wisdom to knowing God, I would like to pose a hypothetical dilemma for people. How many of the world's most educated men and women would be willing to consider their degrees as a pile of rubbish to obtain a simple faith of immeasurable worth in the person of Jesus Christ? The world would understandably reject such an offer with their Christless logic in action. But alas, we have Christians, who, in their pursuit of wisdom and knowledge, have done away with the Author's word and are bewitched by the words of godless professors and gurus of their influence.

At the end of the day, even the most esteemed person's words of wisdom are foolishness to God (1 Cor. 3:18). It is not only secular wisdom that distracts people from seeking God; but also even knowledge of the Holy, if stored up for the sake of knowledge only, can blind one from seeing the true face of the Lord. The latter are those who love the knowledge of God more than they love the person of God. You are called to love the person of Christ and not just the doctrine of Christ. The latter paves the way for the former, where the soul finds its truest and most satisfactory delight.

The Bible asks the question, "Where is the one who is wise? Where is the scribe? Where is the debater of this age? Has not God made foolish the wisdom of the world? For since, in the wisdom of God, the world did not know God through wisdom, it pleased God through the folly of what we preach to save those who believe" (1 Cor. 1:20-21). The recipients of these words should never forget the power of the simple yet profound message that saved them.

When the criteria for who has the authority to preach are based on one's level of formal education instead of his character, we get preaching devoid of power and unction, which sadly plagues many of our churches. For if one's qualification depended on a piece of paper, we might as well hire the greatest of godless minds whose character, vile as it may be, can at least juggle and stretch their words, securing a crowd of spellbound Christians. But know this: inspiration only comes with the Spirit's indwelling and unction when one yields to the Spirit's authority.

The Christian's mission to call the lost to salvation is urgent. In order to rescue souls from the present sinful and adulterous generation, we need believing Christians whose faith is tried and whose character is in continual submission to the Father's pruning, the Son's shepherding, and the Spirit's clothing of power to bear witness of the risen Christ. We can cure an unbelieving world through believing saints who express utmost love and loyalty to the Lord of their salvation. When displayed by the Bride of Christ in all purity while awaiting the Bridegroom's return, all of these attributes will attract people to the Lord of her righteousness and have them wonder who is behind her pure and joyful way of life.

I have heard many sermons preached on the topic of faith, which mostly amounted to a heavy emphasis on exercising one's ability to get things from God rather than get to God. A mature, confident Christian desires God for Who He is; and the more of God that is revealed to him, the more of God he yearns to seek. Until the final moment when faith is turned to sight and prayer to praise, this type of Christian will continue to seek God's face on this side of eternity's shores. Let us believe in what God has said about Who He is because "without faith it is impossible to please him, for whoever would draw near to God must believe that he exists and that he rewards those who seek him" (Heb. 11:6).

Everyone is fine with caution-based faith, which alleviates sacrifice and risks at all costs. I daresay, let a man lay hold of God's word unto complete abandonment of self, you will see the greatest of his supporters, from his family to his friends, turn into the strictest of opposers. The preacher's hand will be foremost in it. One of the greatest examples of faith I read about is of that which belonged to a man from the Bible named Abraham, who "by faith obeyed when he was called to go out to a place that he was to receive as an inheritance. And he went out, not knowing where he was going" (Heb. 11:8).

I can hear many amens shouted at the mention of this Scripture. Now let the wind of the Spirit drive a man to an unplanned, unorganized, and unfathomable place of his calling; and he would be quickly discouraged to move on because of the uncertainty it presents. This is due to the fallen man's tendency to question the supernatural call of God toward the unseen and reduce it down to that which can be seen, touched, and felt. And yet, the promise still stands: "Blessed are those who have not seen and yet have believed" (John 20:29). These words not only speak about faith in the presence of the Lord but also imply our faith in the words of the Lord. The blessing applies to those who believe the word of the Lord over fallible created beings.

Faith that is despised and shunned as fanaticism finds its home in the list of men and women in the Book of Hebrews, chapter eleven. Their logic-defying acts of courage would, like a needle, poke and pop the puffed-up minds of our modern-day comfort-loving and life-preserving preachers and theologians, who spend more time debating about obedience instead of employing themselves to its joyance task. On the other hand, I know of many people who have a voracious appetite for the knowledge of the Bible and are capable of quoting from its pages at any time, if need be. They are quite informed about the doctrinal, historical, and archeological aspects; but sadly, their lofty knowledge of these wonderful truths was not attended with humility.

Instead of bending their knees in gratitude to the Giver of the revelation, many stand proudly, boasting of their intellectual achievements. The current crisis is not merely a knowledge crisis but, more significantly, a crisis of faith. Faith in the word of God, leading to obedience, should be prioritized over faith in the knowledge of the Word, which tends to emphasize intellectual accumulation. After hearing our Lord preach about matters concerning His knowledge of the Father's good pleasure and authority over the kingdom of darkness, "a woman in the crowd raised her voice and said to him, 'Blessed is the womb that bore you, and the breasts at which you nursed!' But He said, 'Blessed rather are those who hear the word of God and keep it'" (Luke 11:27-28).

Before this glorious praise, our Lord was teaching the simplest yet most profound way to pray to the Father. He demonstrated His authority and power over the kingdom of darkness by casting out a demon from a mute man while He taught and exposed the ways of evil spirits toward sinful men. After seeing and hearing the Lord, the woman could not help but burst forth with praise. Notice how our Lord quickly shifts the focus from the praise that is issued from witnessing the fruit of His relationship to the Father and instead emphasizes the true praiseworthy blessing to be found in the hidden roots of faith-filled obedience. This same faith can help believers do the same works that He did and even greater ones, too, because our Lord would send the Holy Spirit to work in the world after He had ascended (John 14:12).

God is after a breed of people who hear His Word and obey it, for this is the only qualification one needs to be used by God. Let us become hearers and keepers of His sacred word. Sadly, our churches, for the most part, are filled with people who are quick to speak but slow to hear. They are packed with individuals who are swift to pile up excuses for disobedience but always hesitant to practice needed obedience. They are faithful in writing sermon notes but faithless when required to act on them and thankful in prosperity but grumblers in showing charity. The secret to receiving God's promises is to have a childlike belief in His promises. Without this faith, you may know about God's promises but never end up securing them.

Look at what Jesus says about children when it comes to faith, for example. "'Who is the greatest in the kingdom of heaven?'" was the question the disciples posed. Calling to him a child, our Lord put him in the midst of them and said, "'Truly, I say to you, unless you turn and become like children, you will never enter the kingdom of heaven. Whoever humbles himself like this child is the greatest in the kingdom of heaven'" (Matt. 18:1-4).

Becoming like a child is not achieved by having a childish mind. It means that one should draw trust, humility, and dependency from a child's simple character. A child is humble because he aims to please his father at all times, which makes him unaware of his own presence. His trust comes from believing every promise made to him by his father without any reservation and dependent because apart from his parents, he can do nothing. In the same way, we trust our Heavenly Father because He always keeps His word and has promised never to leave nor forsake us (Phil. 1:6; Heb. 13:5).

To have this childlike faith, one should be humble. Humbleness seems like a demeaning attribute in a world built on self-betterment and pride. Humility simply means an absence of self, which then enables you to serve God and people without selfish motives (Micah 6:8; Phil. 2:3). Thus, you will become utterly dependent on Him and realize that apart from Him, you can do nothing (John 15:5). Simple trust, humility, and dependency on God are the true essence of a Christian.

This is a call to simple yet sacrificial faith, which will take one through the valley of slander and mountains of misunderstandings. The type of faith that comes under attack is the one that moves toward obedience. Tragically, some of the preachers of our generation only do what they know best, talk many out of its practical embrace, and calm the effort with the usual mechanical and powerless words of assurance. After all, there is always the fear of the pew-dweller becoming more spiritual than the preacher himself. A sermon on faith will be aided with hundreds of amens only with a thousand excuses to follow when the sharp two-edged sword pierces the heart, demanding its usage.

Do you believe, or do you say that you do? Test your willingness to obey the voice of the Lord and reveal the true nature of your faith. Should you be found lacking in faith, "'ask, and it will be given to you'" (Matt. 7:7). For nothing pleases the Father more than to answer a prayer for faith with faith. Here lies the secret to one's spiritual stature: believe always, hear quietly, and obey quickly. While we intellectually pick apart God's Word and debate its relevance for today's culture, God is gathering to Himself the poor who are rich in faith, whose faith-employed hands and feet cannot be bound within our modern-day church structure.

But we must remember that God is in the business of educating the uneducated and empowering the outcasts of society with boldness to bear witness to the gospel. For instance, when scratching their heads with astonishment as to how Peter and John, mere uneducated fishermen, spoke with boldness and words that pierced people's hearts with conviction, we are given the reason, "they had been with Jesus" (Acts 4:13). I implore you to set aside endless chatter and debates about what true faith looks like. Instead, be still and place all your faith in the God Who saved you. Fulfill the call to daily obedience, regardless of how it manifests. By doing this, you are doing the will of your Father in Heaven. "For the kingdom of God does not consist in talk but in power" (1 Cor. 4:20).

CHAPTER 17

WAR FOR THE SOULS OF MEN

"And when the devil had ended every temptation,
he departed from him until an opportune time."

Luke 4:13

THROUGHOUT HISTORY, MANKIND HAS PARTAKEN in countless horror-filled wars. And to make matters worse, the basis for every war has been to feed the relentless desire for power of rulers. One of the subjects I always found fascinating at school was history. Learning about the empires that reigned over vast groups of people, some for centuries, was thrilling. The thing that I found jaw-dropping was the unceasing desire of rulers to conquer the entire world. Every so often, some men—such as Napoleon, Alexander the Great, and Genghis Khan—came very close to doing just that. Those who know their history books have studied and observed the grim outcome of wars and the tragedy they leave in their wake, namely the staggering number of casualties.

While we know all the past and present wars as we have read and seen them in the earthly realms, there is a war with far more significant consequences being waged in the spiritual realm. In this unseen battle, the soul is the battleground; and the devil, along with his demons, prowls the earth, seeking to devour those who are vulnerable. This is a terrifying war where one's eternal abode is determined based on who you pledge your allegiance to. Its origin can be traced before man's creation when the devil and his loyal angels rebelled against God's authority and joined a pact to undo the purity of God's most beloved creation, man.

After the fall of man, the devil, along with his angels, has been permitted to roam the earth, darkening the minds, blinding the eyes, and hardening the hearts of humanity against God. The severity of this spiritual war far surpasses the scale of all human wars that will ever be fought, as earthly battles can only claim the life of the body, while the spiritual batter threatens your eternal soul. The invisible combat being waged in the heavens is kindled by the flames of spiritual forces of evil in the heavenly places. It is a war unseen by mortal eyes. Many are not aware of its effect. Even with its brightest-minded nuclear scientists, the earth cannot produce a weapon strong enough to challenge the evil forces in the demonic spiritual realms. We must know that the power of the flesh is rendered useless when waging war against spiritual beings.

So is mankind doomed to fall under the rule of the evil one? Praise God! The answer is a resounding no because the Son of God came to the earth to destroy the works of the devil (1 John 3:8). To escape the snare of the devil, one must run to the Lord Jesus Christ, Who, through death, has destroyed the devil, who formerly had harnessed the power of death. In addition, by rising from the dead, Jesus ensured that He would deliver all who, through the fear of death, were subject to lifelong slavery (Heb. 2:14).

As Christians, we must be aware of the unseen realm because, to effectively use the weapons of righteousness, one must locate their target for a better aim. No matter how strong the enemy and how great his power is, we must fight this war "with the weapons of righteousness for the right hand and for the left" (2 Cor. 6:7)—mot in the power of the flesh, which will render you useless and end in your defeat. With millions of lost souls who are under the clutches of the flesh, the world, and the devil, could it be that the soldiers of the cross are fast asleep with the armory of God at their disposal, whereas the devil and his destroyers tirelessly plot and execute spells of unawareness over the masses blinded toward eternity? While many in our modern-day churches are quick to embrace the "once saved, always saved" doctrine, I wonder how many are even aware of the possibility of the antithesis of this statement—"once damned, always damned"—is just as equally valid.

Sadly, many gray-haired Christians I have encountered throughout the years are not weaned from the milk of basic biblical concepts like salvation and prayer and are content to remain bare bones in their theology. Conversely, I have seen believers who are relatively new in the faith excel to such incredible heights of sanctification through their humble surrender. As a Christian studies the Scriptures and bends his heart in obedience, the devil and his demons, in a raging fury, will attempt to hinder the progress at all costs, mainly through distractions, which appear non-sinful at the start but sooner or later lead to sin. We have no reason to fear the prowling lion who seeks to intimidate and devour us. Our remedy from his deception is to worship the Victor Who has crushed the head of that cunning dragon. We are clothed with shining array of His righteousness with a promised victory if we continue looking unto "the founder and perfecter of our faith" (Heb. 12:2).

Remember that we fight against the flesh by yielding to the Spirit, and we overcome the world through abiding in the Son Who overcame it. We defeat the devil's accusations by believing the Father's proclamation of the finished work at Calvary. The war for the souls of men is the oldest of all wars, which has primarily been fought in the spiritual realms; and the main objective of this war is to keep the image-bearers separated from the God Who made them. They do so by arousing the passions of the sinful nature of the fallen man, keeping him busy with seeking after that which the sinful flesh desires. The soul that is already lost in its Adam-inherited sinfulness is now twice lost due to obeying its lusts, which is the doing of the powers and principalities under the direct command of their chief, Satan.

And yet, the Christian happens to be the greatest threat to a demon's way of life because God has placed their authority under the Christian's feet.

The subject of their former rule is now made the object of their dread. It is not that the Christian holds in himself the authority over the powers of darkness; but rather, he is a child of the God who has "disarmed the rulers and authorities and put them to open shame, by triumphing over them" (Col. 2:15) by the cross, thus granting the blood-purchased authority to His blood-bought child. Our Lord Jesus Himself confirms the victorious triumph of the Christian over the devils in the following words: "'Behold, I have given you authority to tread on serpents and scorpions, and over all the power of the enemy, and nothing shall hurt you'" (Luke 10:19).

I am afraid that the Church of our day is unaware of the battle at hand. Yet they should be told so that they can fight this war with confidence, knowing that we are on the winning side—that is, if they continue drawing their strength from the Victor Himself and steer clear of the allure of sin that seeks to distract a Christian soldier from the task at hand. For the Word of God urges us as sojourners and exiles to abstain from the passions of the flesh, which wage war against our souls (1 Peter 2:11); and, "let us not sleep, as others do, but let us keep awake and be sober" (1 Thess. 5:6).

All of this is important because a church that is unaware of the ongoing spiritual battle at hand has already declared its defeat. A sleeping soldier is the devil's greatest asset, and he will labor at all costs to get his prey to forsake the watchtower. Consider this: after all the failed attempts of cursing the nation of Israel, Balaam saw that it pleased God to bless Israel. Known for his craftiness, Balaam advised women to lure the men of Israel into worshipping the false Moabite god, Baal, and partaking in the pagan festivities, leading to sexual immorality. The rampant sinning that ensued angered God, Who, in retaliation, sent a plague to the nation of Israel, which killed twenty-four thousand Israelites (Num. 25:1-9, 31:16).

Notice that what started as a mere invitation by the Moabite women quickly became an idolatrous celebration that gave birth to uncontained immorality. Ask yourself, then, how does the enemy attack the blessed and beloved of God? The answer lies in enticing them with what appears to be a harmless invitation that appeals to the desires of the flesh, while diverting their hearts from the commandments of God.

The men who had been so easily seduced to sin by women were warriors who had not long ago defeated the great Amorite kings, Sihon and Og. Just when Israel had reached the pinnacle of victory, these warrior men gave women their honor and strength, who, with their seductive speech, persuaded them to sin. At once, the men followed the women as an ox goes to the slaughter or as a stag is caught fast till an arrow pierces its liver and as a bird rushes into a snare. They marched confidently into the bedchambers of sin, unaware that it would cost them their lives (Prov. 7:21-23). We have the mightiest and the wisest men, like Samson, David, and Solomon, who defeated foreign armies and ruled over nations yet were themselves subdued by lust. In each of these cases, we find that intimacy with the Lord caused them to prosper, keeping their helmets fastened and swords sharpened and their shields clenched. Shockingly, taking a tragic moral stumble, it caused them to bow their head in shame. This now resulting in their bodies being exposed, swords blunted, and shields held limply, which made them easy targets of the evil one.

That being said, I would urge my fellow soldiers to:

> Put on the whole armor of God, that you may be able to stand against the schemes of the devil. For we do not wrestle against flesh and blood, but against the rulers, against the authorities, against the cosmic powers over this present darkness, against the spiritual forces of evil in the heavenly places. Therefore take up the whole armor of God, that you may be able to withstand in the evil day, and having done all, to stand firm. Stand therefore, having fastened on the belt of truth, and having put on the breastplate of righteousness, and, as shoes for your feet, having put on the readiness given by the gospel of peace. In all circumstances take up the shield of faith, with which you can extinguish all the flaming darts of the evil one; and take the

helmet of salvation, and the sword of the Spirit, which is the
word of God, praying at all times in the Spirit, with all prayer
and supplication" (Eph. 6:11-18).

This might very well be one of the most quoted and yet also among the
least applied biblical passages of our time. Thankfully, God has given us the
required armor to withstand the enemy's attacks. We will be victorious as
long as we have the armor on. Always be alert because the darts of deception
and distraction come flying at us when we are found without our armor.
When the enemy swings his sword to undo our faith, we must be found
standing firm in the knowledge of the truth of Christ's triumph over sin,
believing in the impenetrable righteousness of Christ to protect the heart
from all defilement.

We must be ready at all times to evangelize as partakers of the gospel
and recipients of its peace, holding up the faith of the Son of God as our
shield against the fiery attacks of the devil. In addition, we should wear the
helmet of Christ's salvation to protect the mind from all distractions. Finally,
we should unsheathe and learn how to wield the two-edged sword of the
Word of God as our offense against the spiritual forces of evil in the heavenly
places and secure its timely and prevailing usage through constant prayer in
the Spirit.

This equipment and training are necessary because the world is a warzone
for Christians. There is no other way of putting it: spiritual warfare is serious
and should be viewed as such, despite many treating it as a playground. The
spiritual world is where the enemy of all righteousness has made sure to put
landmines, snares, pits, and other traps for pilgrims on the path to eternal
life. "Be sober-minded; be watchful. Your adversary the devil prowls around
like a roaring lion, seeking someone to devour" (1 Peter 5:8).

We have a ruthless enemy who will travel to any lengths to blind and
lead souls to damnation. On top of that, he practices predatory stealth to
seek and devour his prey. Unfortunately, many churches are so naive that

they pet the lion and invite him into their gatherings by resting the shield and sheathing the sword. They handle their spiritual lives in such a playful manner that they themselves become prey. The furthest from the enemy's skillfully crafted deceptions are those who are clothed in battle attire and march in the victory of the cross. To such Christians, the roar of the enemy has no bearing and is quickly drowned out by their loud shouts of praise that silence the devil's lies. Their labor fills the earth with praise and Heaven with souls as they march through this life with the sole purpose of glorifying the conquering Lion of the tribe of Judah, Jesus Christ our Lord.

CHAPTER 18

IT IS A CONVERSION ISSUE

"Having the appearance of godliness, but denying its power. Avoid such people."

2 Timothy 3:5

WE LIVE IN A COUNTRY where the majority have heard the name of Jesus Christ and have been exposed to some of the gospel messages. Still, sadly, there lies a staggering number of unconverted church-attending individuals who bear the title of a Christian yet live contrary to the words of Him they profess to believe. We have cheapened the precious message and immeasurable power of Christ's salvation by holding unconverted masses to the standard of Christianity. I wonder how the early church would react to what passes as today's Christianity. The signs of life in a congregation are not to be judged based on the number of its attendees or the style of worship one renders but rather on one's desire to look like the Lord Jesus Christ. What happens to a man or a woman when indwelt by the Author of life? They live—and live abundantly—for the same Author Who has breathed upon them the new life, joy, and everlasting peace. Not only will the recipient of Christ's salvation feel its earthquake-like soul-shaking transformation, but also, those near will acknowledge the aftermath of its power. Must we not believe the work of the Blessed Spirit who indwelt Christ and raised Him from the dead to likewise raise a damned sinner from their deadness into glorious salvation resulting in eternal life?

What, then, is causing the passionless, non-sacrificial, and world-loving Christianity of our day? The answer is unconverted souls who would like to think of themselves as converted. "Examine yourselves, to see whether you are in the faith. Test yourselves. Or do you not realize this about yourselves, that Jesus Christ is in you? —unless indeed you fail to meet the test" (2 Cor. 13:5). We are quick to assure our people of salvation and slow in pointing people to soul examination to know if the Spirit has wrought true conversion. Have you received "the Spirit of adoption by whom you cry, "'Abba! Father?' The Spirit himself bears witness with our spirit that we are children of God" (Rom. 8:15-16). Do not give yourself any rest until God Almighty Himself assures you of your costly and blood-bought sonship. When it comes to knowing your soul estate, despite doctrinal soundness, rest not upon the words of your preacher nor your heart but upon the words of the sure and steadfast Anchor of your soul, the Lord Jesus Christ, Who "is able to save to the uttermost those who draw near to God through him" (Heb. 7:25). The surety of belonging to God is the sweetest revelation, whereas the affirmation of false security will lead to blinding destruction. By hastening to confirm the work of the Spirit without once displaying the fruit of the Spirit, millions are being led astray as they are told to fall upon the promises of the empty and false security of salvation, the hand of modern-day evangelicals being the foremost.

Witnessing first-hand accounts of multiple individuals, many of whom I personally know and love, walking in the confidence of their baptism, church attendance, and said prayers for a sure entry into Heaven, all the while rejecting the words of the God Whose Heaven they want to inherit, has driven me to many sleepless and speechless nights in prostration. Parents do no favor to their children, or children to their parents, for affirming each party of their salvation, which was never wrought in them. We live in a church age where those pursuing absolute holiness are deemed a threat, yet the very same people will rush to safeguard their souls that are wallowing in their unconverted state. Instead of throwing the rope of Christ's word to snatch the sinking soul caught up in a raging sea, they are encouraged to stay afloat without aid, only waiting to be swallowed up by death that is looming around the corner. We cannot remove the offense of the cross nor its call to complete surrender, and the gospel message is such that it comforts the afflicted and afflicts those living in comfort. How many of our youth are speeding their way to destruction because they trust in what their parents believed was abiding salvation, a belief preserved for reputation and relationship, knowingly or ignorantly? We cannot use the precious mercy of God as a justifier for wicked lifestyles or the grace of God for willful disobedience. The patience and kindness of God are mocked when it is treated as though it were a piece of duct tape applied to cover up our habitual lifestyle of practicing iniquity.

> Everyone who makes a practice of sinning also practices lawlessness; sin is lawlessness. You know that he appeared in order to take away sins, and in him there is no sin. No one who abides in him keeps on sinning; no one who keeps on sinning has either seen him or known him. Little children, let no one deceive you. Whoever practices righteousness is righteous, as he is righteous. Whoever makes a practice of sinning is of the devil, for the devil has been sinning from the beginning. The reason the Son of God appeared was to destroy the works of the devil. No one born of God makes a practice of sinning, for God's seed abides in him; and he cannot keep on sinning, because he has been born of God. By this it is evident who are the children of God, and who are the children of the devil: whoever does not practice righteousness is not of God, nor is the one who does not love his brother (1 John 3:4-10).

God's children are those who love and practice righteousness, even as their Lord is righteous. On the other hand, the children of the devil are those who love and practice sin, even as their lord, who has been sinning from the beginning. "No one," says the blessed Holy Spirit, "born of God makes a practice of sinning" (1 John 3:9). Indeed, he cannot because Christ has made His home in that man's heart. In other words, the soul that makes a practice of sin is unconverted because Christ cannot and will not live in a vessel infested with iniquity. A Christian who stumbles in sin is not to be likened unto them who willingly plunge themselves into its lifestyle. Brokenness leading to anguished repentance and separates the stumbling believer from the cold and unmoved condition of the unconverted individual. I believe that the crime of the century is preachers and evangelists of our day consoling the lost of their wickedness and confronting the saved for their holiness. What would happen if an oncologist, in his attempt to avoid the patient's displeasure and speechless reaction, hid the truth of a newly detected cancer inside the patient's body? It would gradually spread and lead to certain death.

In the same way, the Christian must speak the truth to save lives, no matter the fury it invites. "That is very unloving for you to say," said no one to a doctor when diagnosed with cancer or other life-threatening diseases. Rather, after gathering themselves together due to the nature of the news, the patient is already found consulting with the doctor about the treatments without delay. How much more should the Christian, who knows the root cause of all sickness, speak the truth to those on the verge of perdition? Doctors can only treat the physical needs of the sick, but the Christian has the answers to cure the spiritual sickness of the lost. The light of the gospel exposes the darkness of sin; and if we truly believe the power of the gospel, we must unapologetically speak its truth, which sets free the captives from sin's dominion. We must also warn about the devastating effects of sin, which blinds the eyes and hardens the heart to the saving message of the gospel. "Not everyone who says to me, 'Lord, Lord,' will enter the kingdom of heaven, but the one who does the will of my Father who is in heaven. On that day many will say to me, 'Lord, Lord, did we not prophesy in your name, and cast out demons in your name, and do many mighty works in your name?' And then will I declare to them, 'I never knew you; depart from me, you workers of lawlessness'" (Matt. 7:21-23).

Ask yourself, is God your Father? So what if you believe that God is one, for so do the demons (James 2:19)? The more pressing question to ask is this: are you doing the Father's will? For the will of God concerning salvation is "that everyone who looks on the Son and believes in him should have eternal life" (John 6:40). Sanctification follows from saving faith, leading to more Christlikeness and abstinence from that which is evil and displeasing to God (1 Peter 2:15; 1 Thess. 4:3-8, 5:18). You may call Him Lord and convince yourself to be a Christian because you have done all you can to appear as such, from prophesying to casting out demons and many other mighty works, all in the name of the Lord. Yet the Lord says, "'I never knew you'" (Matt. 7:23). The works that appeared spiritual were all done in one's name while taking Christ's name to spiritualize and cover up their lawless deeds.

Rightfully, does the Lord call such men and women "'workers of lawlessness.'" The Lord tells us that we will recognize them by their fruits; and we prove to be the Lord's disciple when we bear much fruit, which brings glory to the Father (Matt. 7:15-20; John 15:8). And the fruit of fruits that is at display for all to see is the Christian's love for each other even as the Lord loved us by sacrificially laying down His life for us, by which we echo to the world our message of belonging to the Lord Jesus Christ (John 13:34-35). And this holy and sacrificial love of God which is in Christ Jesus our Lord is that which "does not rejoice at wrongdoing, but rejoices with the truth" (1 Cor. 13:6). God's love can only be treasured by those who have wholly surrendered their lives to the God of love. Would you rather not allow the words of love to offend and grieve you into repenting on this side of eternity, where there is mercy in abundance, instead of finding yourself at the judgment seat of God, only to stagger at the mercy ignored when on earth?

Let us now turn our attention toward those who would excuse themselves from their Christian duties while imposing the same upon others. The Word of God is loud and clear about this matter, and let us hear it in the words of the apostle Paul himself:

Therefore you have no excuse, O man, every one of you who judges. For in passing judgment on another you condemn yourself, because you, the judge, practice the very same things. We know that the judgment of God rightly falls on those who practice such things. Do you suppose, O man—you who judge those who practice such things and yet do them yourself—that you will escape the judgment of God? Or do you presume on the riches of his kindness and forbearance and patience, not knowing that God's kindness is meant to lead you to repentance? But because of your hard and impenitent heart you are storing up wrath for yourself on the day of wrath when God's righteous judgment will be revealed. He will render to each one according to his works: to those who by patience in well-doing seek for glory and honor and immortality, he will give eternal life; but for those who are self-seeking and do not obey the truth, but obey unrighteousness, there will be wrath and fury. There will be tribulation and distress for every human being who does evil, the Jew first and also the Greek, but glory and honor and peace for everyone who does good, the Jew first and also the Greek. For God shows no partiality (Rom. 2:1-11).

It is easier to convince a heathen of his unconverted nature than to deal with those who think themselves converted yet are Christless as some tribal heathens. Did you know that a Christian, a true one, is one who sets an example of godliness through his loving obedience to the word of his Father in Heaven? "Therefore whoever relaxes one of the least of these commandments and teaches others to do the same will be called least in the kingdom of heaven, but whoever does them and teaches them will be called great in the kingdom of heaven" (Matt. 5:19). There are those who say they believe, but their actions prove otherwise. Remember, one must be a believer, a doer, and then a teacher; for all three need to be followed to reap effectiveness.

Just as the apostle Paul accused the Jews of dishonoring God by violating the very law in which they took such pride, this act tarnished God's testimony among unbelievers, as he states: "The name of God is blasphemed among the

Gentiles because of you" (Rom. 2:24). In the same way, there are Christians whose boasting in the gospel is brought to naught due to their handling of its call, namely obedience as a result of faith. And with such acts of hypocrisy, we continue to dishonor the very Name of whose gospel we proclaim. He who treats the implication of the gospel lightly is sure to have never believed; for there is not a single soul on the face of the whole earth, past and present, whom the Holy Spirit indwelt without leading their thoughts and desires toward the commands of Christ. No, not one!

The reason many in our day are more interested in the perishables from earth's nest is that they have never tasted the eternal glory of Heaven's best. Our Lord Jesus died to save us from that which held us captive, namely sin, and to empower the believer to continue living the new life in the blood-bought and Spirit-filled power of the resurrected life. Bring all the deadness of sin and come to the altar in complete surrender, and you will behold the saving power of the gospel. Yes, you can live in victory over every bondage of sin, despite what your preacher would have you believe. There is enough power in the blood of the Lamb to cleanse, purify, and quicken a sinner into a saint. Ah! "Are you implying that we can live a sinless life?" would then be the question of many. It is not sinless life at talk here but the holy and unstained life Christ died to bestow upon His Bride. A life of victory over sin, albeit life's tribulations and sin's temptations, is still a glorious life nonetheless because with us is the conquering Lamb, through whom we will likewise overcome and one day take off the battle armor as we step into glory.

CHAPTER 19

JUDGMENT IS HERE

"And he said with a loud voice, 'Fear God and give him glory,
because the hour of his judgement has come, and worship him who made
heaven and earth, the sea and the springs of water.'"

Revelation 14:7

ONE OF THE MOST DESPISED words in the Christian culture of our day is the word *judgment*, especially the one from God. We live in a nation that has not only tasted God's goodness but has also sent hundreds and thousands of missionaries to proclaim the goodness of God to nations near and far. Many of these missionaries gave up their comforts and instead chose to wed suffering because the Christ they believed in was not worshiped in the distant jungles of the Amazon to the desolate villages of Africa and all the way to the slums in Asia. How did we transition from the blessedness of receiving and spreading the light of the gospel into a nation that now suppresses the very source of its blessings, inviting upon itself the curses of ungodliness and the darkness of Christless legislations? I owe a heavy debt of gratitude to the United States for playing an instrumental role in my Christian pilgrimage. Therefore, as the Almighty bears me witness, I will allow my broken heart to testify about my love for this once great nation.

It is not so much about what America did in the past as much as what she is doing today that will determine her future in God's scales. The same applies to England, Australia, and Canada. The impenitent invites the judgment of

God, whether an individual or a nation. We must awaken ourselves from the theology that likes to believe "all is well," leading to abandoning everything concerning the mounting spiritual crisis of our present day. It has admitted many good-natured Christians into a spiritual coma that portrays the world and the human race as worthy of honor and undeserving of God's judgment. Perhaps the pages of history will refresh our forgetful minds of all the nations, including the nation of Israel, who joined themselves in doing evil. As a result, they brought the judgment of sword, famine, pestilence, and captivity upon themselves. But there was, is, and always will be resistance against the message of judgment because it calls for a swift, heart-rending, action-amending, and knee-bending type of response, which is a direct affront to a disobedient child of Adam. The Lord Jesus Christ stands ready to judge both the living and the dead; wherefore, neglecting to warn the masses headed to Christless judgment will be a crime of a grand scale. If judgment starts in the Church of God, I am sure judgment will also start and has already begun with nations who have waived the banner of Christianity for centuries yet are defiantly breaking, practicing, and advertising abominable deeds contrary to the law of its Author.

"For when your judgments are in the earth, the inhabitants of the world learn righteousness" (Isa. 26:9). There is always a just reason for the God of Heaven to bring judgment upon an ungodly world. We see this in Abraham's persistent intercession before God to spare the righteous in Sodom, to which God responds by promising to spare the city for the sake of the fifty, forty, thirty, twenty, and even ten righteous people should they be found in it (Gen. 18:23-33). But tragically, there was only one righteous man who lived among them, tormenting his righteous soul over the lawless deeds of the Sodomites (2 Peter 2:8), even Lot whom God spared according to His abundant mercy, along with his family.

We see that God always spares the righteous because they trust in His righteousness and are zealous for its spread. If you fall upon God's mercy, judgment will pass over you; but if you continue to live in the goodness of your unredeemed character, judgment will overtake you. "'Truly, truly, I say to you, whoever hears my word and believes him who sent me has eternal life. He does not come into judgment, but has passed from death to life'" (John 5:24). The Son of God is the world's only sure escape from the coming judgment of the wrath and fury of the Father toward a Christ-rejecting world. To escape the coming judgment, the Almighty declares that you must "Kiss the Son, lest he be angry, and you perish in the way, for his wrath is quickly kindled. Blessed are all who take refuge in him" (Psalm 2:12).

The Lord of Heaven has full rights over the earth He created and can, at any time, bring into existence or take away any creature without needing their permission. Besides, the God Whose throne is founded upon justice and righteousness (Psalm 89:14) is not obligated to inform and explain His unfathomable ways to an unrighteous man because "evil men do not understand justice, but those who seek the LORD understand it completely" (Prov. 28:5). Can anyone look at the current world events with a sober mind and not discern that judgment is already unfolding in the form of nations threatening other nations with total nuclear annihilation? It causes leaders to speed up their centuries-long plan to usher in a new world of prosperity and security with a new religion under the guise of unity and peace, only to hype up the masses to render worship to the Antichrist for its fruition at his revelation.

"For the one who sows to his own flesh will from the flesh reap corruption, but the one who sows to the Spirit will from the Spirit reap eternal life" (Gal. 6:8). Decades of sowing into Antichrist-like ideologies and practices have birthed despicable corruption in our society, which only calls for the judgment of like proportion according to history. The grim practice of abortion will bring about the downfall of any society, despite a nation's speedy advancement in social and economic reformation. When innocent lives are considered worthy of slaughter, veiled under the umbrella of professionalism, know that judgment has already come. Everything starts with life, and God especially deems humans infinitely more precious than other creatures. Therefore, its handling will dictate the value that is placed upon it. Lack of discernment has resulted in many falling victim to the so-called professionals and experts of our day, whose practice shadows that of the worshipers of Baal, then that of the Author and Sustainer of life whose nation we are supposedly under. The judgment upon nations that never acknowledged Christian faith would be far lesser in comparison to those who took the name of Christ to fulfill their lustful desires.

The ongoing and unmentionable devilish practices in many developed societies directly result from the masses rejecting God's authority. It is an attempt of a sinful man to elevate his desires that spew unrighteousness over the words of God, "who desires all people to be saved and to come to the knowledge of the truth" (1 Tim. 2:4). Woe to America, England, Canada, and Australia; for if the mighty works done in you had been done in Sodom and Gomorrah, they would've long ago repented in sackcloth and ashes. With innumerable Christian resources, countless seminaries with top intellectual minds, and staggering access to jaw-dropping funds, we are getting judged and headed into further judgment for wearing pride as our necklace while continuing to unashamedly deck our fading accomplishments with ornaments of human praise. "Blessed is the nation whose God is the Lord," and on the flip side, cursed it is when it forgets the source of its blessing (Psalm 33:12; Psalm 9:17). How can we continue to sing, "God Bless the USA," and curse the same God by approving the many things He hates?

God is getting ready to deploy the Jonahs of the last days to herald the message of faith, repentance, and judgment before the outstretched arms of mercy are withdrawn and the fury of His wrath is poured out. When a nation approves, distributes, and partakes in iniquity from the highest places of influence, starting from the revered halls of the Supreme Court to the office of the Congress, all the way to the corridors of your state legislators' offices, its survival is under looming destruction. Let your unbelieving mind observe and unconverted heart grasp the outcome of historic nations that were at one time lavished with unfathomable power and prosperity. They were destroyed in a matter of days because they continued to promote laws and lifestyles which called evil, good, and good, evil; which put darkness for light and light for darkness; which put bitter for sweet and sweet for bitter.

For example, let us consider Rome an untouchable powerhouse until God decided to pull the plug. The same thing happened to ancient Assyria, Babylon, Persia, Greece, and above all, the very nation of Israel, which God Himself delivered over to famine, sword, pestilence, and captivity due to their unrepentant heart. Where is God's mercy in all of this, you may ask, to which I would reply, "In the very question itself, since you are given the breath, time, and opportunity to ask for it." God will never, ever, reject a truly repentant heart, for He reveals to such the promise of abundant pardon and salvation. Let us then, "Fear God and keep his commandments, for this is the whole duty of man. For God will bring every deed into judgment, with every secret thing, whether good or evil" (Eccl. 12:13-14).

Hear and fear, oh exultant rulers of the earth, and marvel at the majesty of the God of Heaven, Whose authority and power govern and rule over all the kingdoms under Heaven, which are best described in the words of the prophet Isaiah: "Behold, the nations are like a drop from a bucket, and are accounted as the dust on the scales; behold, he takes up the coastlands like fine dust. Lebanon would not suffice for fuel, nor are its beasts enough for a burnt offering. All the nations are as nothing before him, they are accounted by him as less than nothing and emptiness" (Isa. 40:15-17).

> It is he who sits above the circle of the earth, and its inhabitants are like grasshoppers; who stretches out the heavens like a curtain, and spreads them like a tent to dwell in; who brings princes to nothing, and makes the rulers of the earth as emptiness. Scarcely are they planted, scarcely sown, scarcely has their stem taken root in the earth, when he blows on them, and they wither, and the tempest carries them off like stubble (Isa. 40:22-24).

CHAPTER 20

HOW THEN SHALL WE LIVE

"The spirit of man is the lamp of the Lord, searching all his innermost parts."

Proverbs 20:27

TO THE CHRISTIAN WHO ENTIRELY agrees with the words of our Lord Jesus Christ and who has uttered a thousand amens while reading this literature thus far, let me ask you a question. While you may hold on to the teachings of the Bible and possess prestigiously sound theology, are you displaying your unwavering commitment by your solemn approach to the obedience of the words you confess to have believed? While you are quick to point out the sins of others, have you deeply examined your ways in light of the words that are likened unto a lamp that guides your feet as you walk the path set before you (Psalm 119:105)? You may have also publicly refuted heresies and called many sinners to repentance, but do you recall offering brokenness and tears at the altar of intercession for the straying sinner? Being raised with Christian morals and instructed in the ways of righteousness, you have heaped up a wealth of knowledge and stored up instructions. If trials and tribulations were to threaten and squeeze the life out of an individual of your caliber with unmatched spiritual attainments, would one discover the sweet fruit of perseverance or an attitude likened to the bitterness of wormwood?

You condemn the slaughter of innocent children as you sigh over the abominable practice of abortion and even vote in accordance with godly principles to uphold the traditional views of marriage, sexuality, and other pressing cultural issues of our time. However, do you allow your voice, passion, and disdain to spread beyond the containment of your homes and secret church meetings? Although Jesus Christ may be your Lord and Savior, are you courageous enough to take a stand and declare Him the Lord and Savior of all in front of a crowd of hissing mockers? I ask these questions because the call of ministry is for those who are as bold as a lion. God's call for every born-again believer is to proclaim the gospel message of Christ's salvation, always being prepared to make a defense to anyone who asks the Christian for a reason for the hope that is in them.

Always, remembering to "do it with gentleness and respect, having a good conscience, so that, when you are slandered, those who revile your good behavior in Christ may be put to shame" (1 Peter 3:15-16). Many cheerleaders in our pulpits today would rather watch the battle from the sidelines than get involved themselves. What I mean by that is that the millions of supposed believers who attend weekly church services and are well acquainted with the crises that plague the Christless world are only found nodding their heads in solemn disappointment. Even though they know that something urgently important is missing from the Church, they only express their displeasure with the passionate shouting of many amens to the weekly news update issued from the pulpit. Compare that to the Church in the Book of Acts, and you will invite upon yourself an embarrassing blush. Unrestrained iniquity reigns due to believers' restrained passion. Because of this, the seemingly impossible has happened; and wickedness has found a voice in the light because the Church has lost hers somewhere in the process of rescuing souls from the darkness. Oh, what have we allowed ourselves to become as a Christian church?

Are you aware that a Shaolin monk in the mountain heights of China, a Shinto Buddhist in the eastern slopes of Japan, and a Hindu priest from the Ganges of India offer their lives freely to practice rituals unto unattainable perfection to an unreachable deity? And then, we have America and other prosperous nations, where we find ourselves pleading and even begging other believers to offer their lives to the God "who did not spare his own Son but gave him up for us all" (Rom. 8:32)—His one and only, pure and precious Holy Son! And for what? Oh, how I blush with embarrassment to see the heathens more zealous in the spread of their religion than a Christian in the Western world. This cannot be the response of a believer in whom Christ lives because, according to the word, when one is born of the Spirit, it is no longer the old fallen person that lives but Christ who lives in the crucified man. The old ways of sin are nailed to the cross and shed away by death to sin, and the person rises from their grave as a new creation in Christ. What a wonderful gift God has given many throughout history. What could one possibly offer back up to God?

Simply put, "God loves a cheerful giver" (2 Cor. 9:7); and the offering of your life is at the pinnacle of all offerings that He desires. When you thus cheerfully place yourself at His disposal, your worship is then accepted and the work of your hands blessed. Your heart then becomes the altar and God's love the flame. It is then filled with the newness of life and holy desires, and the entirety of your being will submit to its new Author. If our Lord Jesus came into the world to make the Father and Himself known, then souls who come to Him must do so with only one goal in view: to know God and Jesus Christ, Whom He sent.

The vessels who carry the gospel message must be wholly surrendered to the Word of God because for God to work in your life, you must embrace the fullness of His authority over your life. God weighs the heart and tests the motive of a man. He knows everything about you that there is to know. Your hidden thoughts within and acts without are visibly observed by the eyes that keep "watch on the evil and the good" (Prov. 15:3). Will those eyes not compel you to live with the highest level of integrity and honesty?

Oh, Christian, the time has come for you to start living the life your Lord died to freely give, one of whole-hearted worship. In this age of social media, numerous social influencers have arisen whose advertisements of iniquity would make even the perverse inhabitants of Sodom and Gomorrah cringe in disgust. But where, oh where, are the gospel influencers of our society? On their journey to try and conquer the shameful and sinful societal practices, weak, so-called believers have fallen prey to its influence, becoming conquered themselves. To move this generation toward God, we would do well to look beyond today's computerized Christians wedded to technology. We must start looking for a breed of Samaritans who are baptized with love and wedded to action, whose compassion stretches beyond the doors of their lips and onto a bruised and bloodied world filled with sin's captives.

As an outsider to our present-day's church culture, such Spirit-crafted prophets are not acquainted with the art of boasting and are void of all pedigree. They would much rather display their provenance by leading souls through their obedient trails to the foot of the cross of Calvary. It starts with you, oh reader; and unless you take up the call to crucify your excuses, your excuses will crucify the call. If the call to worship is a burdensome task and willfully neglected, I implore you to beg for God's mercy so that a new pair of eyes may be given to you and for your ears to be opened and your heart made to desire righteousness. Do not be content with only a superficial understanding of God.

I beseech you to earnestly pray for the eyes to see the tears and blood flowing with great agony, each drop a testament to a love so profound and precious that it gave everything to bring you close. Plead for the ears to hear the voice of the One crying for the forgiveness of His tormentors as your hand was chief in nailing Him to that tree. Beg for a heart to be given, that would treasure a sacrifice so unmerited that it is something even a true friend would seldom give to another. Marvel at this, the Son of God did just that to purchase the worst of His enemies. Will you not ask for such a glorious revelation of the cross? Or will you continue to push away the greatest love, peace, guilt, and sin offering that the merciful Father in Heaven has provided to all so that they could be reconciled to Himself? "For you know the grace of our Lord Jesus Christ, that though he was rich, yet for your sake he became poor, so that you by his poverty might become rich" (2 Cor. 8:9). Oh, what a beautiful and perfectly all-powerful God that we have!

Dare to consider this, dear reader: the eternal glory of Jesus's heavenly throne was laid aside in exchange for over thirty years of toil, poverty, and humiliation just to bring His sheep back into the sheepfold. So, awake, oh soldier, you have been nesting under the umbrella of fireless Christianity, which has placed you in a cold and contented area of indifference! It has deceived you into believing that your present spiritual condition is the highest plateau that can be reached as a Christian, as though there were no further heights to be gained. Even before you start asking yourself questions like, "Is such a life worth it," why don't you begin rightly by asking, "Is He worth it?" Once you are convinced about the Lord's worthiness, the life lived under His loving guidance will be done joyfully and triumphantly.

There is no denying that the cost of carrying your cross is a grueling experience but will be worth it when you stand amazed at the reward of your labor, the precious smile of the Holy One. With that in mind, it is not necessarily what you gain in eternity that will amaze you as much as Who you gain for all eternity. There is so much of God to know, love, and delight in if we would only, in Spirit and truth, bring our hearts near to Him in pure and selfless worship. The following prayer of the psalmist should be our prayer if we must have our path filled with the Word's illumination and our soul with the blessed Holy Spirit's guidance. Even with faith the size of a mustard seed, let us cry out these words to God: "Send out your light and your truth; let them lead me; let them bring me to your holy hill and to your dwelling! Then I will go to the altar of God, to God my exceeding joy, and I will praise you with the lyre, O God, my God" (Psalm 43:3-4).

This precious prayer was fulfilled two thousand years ago during the incredible moment when God sent His Son, Jesus Christ, to be the light for the blind, the truth for the deceived, and the way for the lost. And because of Christ's sacrifice on the cross, we are now made to dwell with Him in the heavenly places. And by the power of faith, Christ lives in our hearts. As God becomes the Source of our exceeding joy, our hearts become the altar of His praise. I believe the only way to be taken higher in the spiritual realm is to continue looking and seeking the glory of the Highest. To be helped by God, you must acknowledge your utter helplessness and fall wholly upon His mercy, which strengthens the weak arm and makes strong the feeble knee.

If you present yourself to the Lord with humble repentance, He will shower you with abundant forgiveness. God is always ready to show mercy to those who humbly see their need for it. Being a fellow beggar of God's mercy, I beg you not to disregard these words of exhortation because, for some of you, these words could be the last that you will hear before you stand trial at the judgment seat of Christ. Come, therefore, all of you who are weary, thirsty, and hungry; and the Lord will give you rest, quench your thirst, and satisfy your hunger. Amen.

CHAPTER 21

REVIVAL WILL COME

"Will you not revive us again, that your people may rejoice in you."

Psalm 85:6

THERE IS A REVIVAL APPROACHING, but not in the way many of us have dreamed of it. I don't believe it will come through catchy church advertisements, well-crafted visions from mainstream Christian organizations, or the strutting pulpits of our day. Instead, I am convinced that the revival for this day will be issued through a handful of Spirit-revived and unknown men and women, carrying in themselves the burden that the majority do not wish for, the impending reality for the unrepentant sinner. Their lives exist for a singular purpose: to spread the passion for the Lord's glory, kindling the torch of awakening in the process. One person under the complete influence of the blessed Holy Spirit has often been the instrument of God's awakening, and the history of the Church speaks to this. Before the Spirit's outpouring on the day of Pentecost, 120 disciples gathered in one place to worship the one true God.

I do not claim to be an expert on the topic of revival like most of the scholars of our day, but the Word of God in me attests to the aftermath of such an event. Take, for example, the influence of certain men such as Ezra, Elijah, King Josiah, King Hezekiah, and John the Baptist, who, although called to different offices, left a trail of obedience that included educating the people in the Word of God. They broke down idols and reformed the temple, waking the slumbering nation of Israel to the God Who burst their bonds of slavery and, above all, calling men and women to repentance. Their passion, the likes of which only a few have attained, was given to them through the singleness of heart in seeking after the passion of the Glory of Israel. And let us not forget the greatest Revivalist and the inspirer of the words of the aforementioned names, the Lord Jesus Christ. Being the Son of God, He could have exercised His Divine powers to subject souls unto Himself. Still, He chose to blaze the road of His Divine influence by setting an example of an intimate relationship with the Father. We are given the reason for the Father's abiding presence with the Son in the following words of the Son Himself: "'For I always do the things that are pleasing to him'" (John 8:29).

Sacrifice is the key that unlocks the door to success. The only ones to enter through those doors are men who want revival at the expense of health, wealth, and even daily bread. If it were true that we had some thousands of appointed revivalists, prophets, and apostles in the United States, contrary to their accepted portrayal by the majority, their faces would have made it to the front covers of the newspapers and headlines over every news channel. They will not be hailed as heroes but jailed as criminals. Most of our preachers are completely unwilling and unprepared for self-crucifixion, let alone act for the cause of revival. These are the men whose churches are filled with scores of unrevived attendees seeking revival on national and international levels while gladly remaining in the state of spiritual stasis. How can you wish the fires of revival to spread while your Christianity stays frozen without fervency?

The Spirit of God kindles revival in the hearts of God's people to turn them to the love of God, thus equipping the people to God's service for the glory of God. Broken repentance is the language of revival. Without repentance, there is no revival; and without revival, the Church remains in the stage of continual relapse. The soul that realizes the need for revival does good, but he that restlessly pursues it will do even better because they are the ones who, through persistence, prevail over the gates of drowsiness and, with toil, secure the souls bound in its untouched chambers of comfort.

When you have secular psychologists more in touch with mankind's ongoing moral crisis, the younger generation seeking spiritual advice from mediums, self-help gurus held in high esteem by the masses, and religious zealots of paganism displaying more passion in the practice of their faith boasting of having more converts than our current evangelical churches, we know the Church desperately needs a revival.

The passionate Church is intimate with God; and as a result, she is unstained by the world, whereas, the apathetic church replicates the world, inviting the chains of incarceration upon herself. I believe that if judgment begins at the house of God, so does revival. Our effectiveness as a Church depends on the level of our awareness of God's presence. The vessels of God's revival always emerge from the most unsuspecting place, people, and position. Take, for example, Ezra, a scribe of the Word of God whose body, on the one hand, is subject to the tyrannical laws of Babylonia. Yet, on the other hand, his soul pants after God and desires to teach and lead the disheartened people of Israel on the highway of holiness. "For Ezra had set his heart to study the Law of the LORD, and to do it and to teach his statutes and rules in Israel" (Ezra 7:10). The result of declaring and expounding the Word of God to a large group of downtrodden people of God resulted in revived worship. Let us read the following account:

> And all the people gathered as one man into the square before the Water Gate. And they told Ezra the scribe to bring the Book of the Law of Moses that the Lord had commanded Israel. So Ezra the priest brought the Law before the assembly, both men and women and all who could understand what they heard, on the first day of the seventh month. And he read from it facing the square before the Water Gate from early morning until midday, in the presence of the men and the women and those who could understand. And the ears of all the people were attentive to the Book of the Law.
>
> And Ezra the scribe stood on a wooden platform that they had made for the purpose. And Ezra opened the book in the sight of all the people, for he was above all the people, and as he opened

it all the people stood. And Ezra blessed the Lord, the great God, and all the people answered, "Amen, Amen," lifting up their hands. And they bowed their heads and worshiped the Lord with their faces to the ground. Also, Jeshua, Bani, Sherebiah, Jamin, Akkub, Shabbethai, Hodiah, Maaseiah, Kelita, Azariah, Jozabad, Hanan, Pelaiah, the Levites, helped the people to understand the Law, while the people remained in their places. They read from the book, from the Law of God, clearly, and they gave the sense, so that the people understood the reading.

And Nehemiah, who was the governor, and Ezra the priest and scribe, and the Levites who taught the people said to all the people, "This day is holy to the LORD your God; do not mourn or weep." For all the people wept as they heard the words of the Law. Then he said to them, "Go your way. Eat the fat and drink sweet wine and send portions to anyone who has nothing ready, for this day is holy to our Lord. And do not be grieved, for the joy of the LORD is your strength." So the Levites calmed all the people, saying, "Be quiet, for this day is holy; do not be grieved." And all the people went their way to eat and drink and to send portions and to make great rejoicing, because they had understood the words that were declared to them (Neh. 8:1-12).

But to have an Ezra-like revival, we need men with Ezra-like characters who are submitted to the Word of God before devoting their lives to its teaching. For the revival of such a national level to take place, there must come an awakening on a personal level, the likes of which we read in the story of King Josiah. Under the kingship of Josiah, revival came through rediscovering the words of life, which the former priests, under the influence of idolatry, allowed its burial and chose to remain unmoved by its absence in their lives. "When the king heard the words of the Book of the Law, he tore his clothes" (2 Kings 22:11), to which God responds with the following:

Because your heart was penitent, and you humbled yourself before the LORD, when you heard how I spoke against this place and against its inhabitants, that they should become a desolation and a curse, and you have torn your clothes and wept before me, I also have heard you, declares the LORD. Therefore, behold, I will gather you to your fathers, and you shall be gathered to your grave in peace, and your eyes shall not see all the disaster that I will bring upon this place. And they brought back word to the king (2 Kings 22:19-20).

Immediately after this, the king gathered the whole nation before the temple of the Lord:

And he read in their hearing all the words of the Book of the Covenant that had been found in the house of the LORD. And the king stood by the pillar and made a covenant before the LORD, to walk after the LORD and to keep his commandments and his testimonies and his statutes with all his heart and all his soul, to perform the words of this covenant that were written in this book. And all the people joined in the covenant (2 Kings 23:2-3).

This revived king, along with those whose hearts God had touched, journeyed to cleanse and rid the nation of all idolatry, beginning from the temple of the Lord. An awakening of this stature, which generates passion for God's glory and holy indignation against every form of idolatry, is gravely needed for this generation of believers, especially among the unmoved audiences of Sunday's meetings. Also, we should pray that it would start from our pulpits.

The fires of revival will not descend upon those seeking after anything except God and Him alone. Passion for evangelism only comes from your devotion to God. Let us recall the story of King Hezekiah, who was appointed as the King of Judah after his father, Ahaz. Unlike his father's abominable practices of idolatry, which even led to child sacrifice, Hezekiah, by the mercy of God, was won over to the Lord of righteousness. One would assume that this newly appointed king would start the reformation of his nation by strengthening the military, building fortresses, and securing as many weapons as possible to defend the nation from foreign enemies, especially Syria and Israel, who were at war with Judah at the time. Unlike the former kings of Judah, Hezekiah starts his reign by opening the temple's doors, which his father had shut, ridding it of impurity and restoring the purity of worship. And this he started in the first year and the first month of his reign. Here is the scriptural account of the event:

> In the first year of his reign, in the first month, he opened the doors of the house of the LORD and repaired them. He brought in the priests and the Levites and assembled them in the square on the east and said to them, "Hear me, Levites! Now consecrate yourselves, and consecrate the house of the LORD, the God of your fathers, and carry out the filth from the Holy Place. For our fathers have been unfaithful and have done what was evil in the sight of the LORD our God. They have forsaken him and have turned away their faces from the habitation of the LORD and turned their backs. They also shut the doors of the vestibule and put out the lamps and have not burned incense or offered burnt offerings in the Holy Place to the God of Israel. Therefore, the wrath of the LORD came on Judah and Jerusalem, and he has made them an object of horror, of astonishment, and of hissing, as you see with your own eyes. For behold, our fathers have fallen by the sword, and our sons and our daughters and our wives are in captivity for this. Now it is in my heart to make a covenant with the LORD, the God of Israel, in order that his fierce anger may turn away from us. My sons, do not now be negligent, for the LORD has chosen you to stand in his presence, to minister to him and to be his ministers and make offerings to him (2 Chron. 29:3-11).

Not only was the king passionate about God's glory, but he was just as much devoted to orderly worship. After reinstituting the long-forsaken

Passover festival and restoring the priestly order of the temple worship, the revival that had descended in the hearts of the true worshippers through pure worship would further spread in the form of zealous cleansing of the nation's idolatry. Here is the forementioned account: "Now when all this was finished, all Israel who were present went out to the cities of Judah and broke in pieces the pillars and cut down the Asherim and broke down the high places and the altars throughout all Judah and Benjamin, and in Ephraim and Manasseh, until they had destroyed them all. Then all the people of Israel returned to their cities, every man to his possession" (2 Chron. 31:1). While many are promoting new techniques and ways to usher revival, we need to get back to the ancient highway of holiness, which Ezra, Josiah, and Hezekiah trod upon. Heaven-sent revival will only come when we like them, open the unpopular and non-trendy doors of ancient worship prescribed according to God's Word in God's way.

The holy remnants are the revived remnants, and the revived remnants will be the instrument of revival to an unholy world. It is through them that God will demonstrate His power. Sadly, some people marvel at the past supernatural outpouring and working of the Spirit on the Day of Pentecost while displaying a dismissive attitude toward the same Spirit's like-natured work in the present. God educates the uneducated, and the educated throughout church history have laid low their degrees and other achievements to sit at the feet of the One "in whom are hidden all the treasures of wisdom and knowledge" (Col. 2:3). The coming revival will not be carried under any denominational or organizational backing. It will not come under the charismatics or the cessationists, a celebrity preacher or your favorite podcaster, but through the praying remnant who suffer much in the place of intercession for their nation and, above all, the purity of the Church. Let us seek to be a part of this remnant who carry in themselves the torch to kindle the hearts of those who are at ease in Zion.

His presence they esteem lightly while His power they desire,

His work throughout church history and the inspired word they admire;

Now let any man so as much His precious gifts inquire,

Swiftly to be talked out of its pursuit, deemed as false fire;

Not knowing the Giver, there are those who envy His gifts, yet against His Word conspire,

Boastful tongues, flattering lips, false prophesies in His name, making Him out to be a liar;

His power and inspiration they claim, while the flesh is the supplier,

"Thus says the Lord" is but a cover-up for them to mammon acquire;

Gifts and graces, He freely bestows upon whom He wills,

What precedes them is holiness in the person He fills;

Impart O blessed Spirit, your incorruptible holy gifts,

Signs and wonders, as your word declares, your glory uplifts;

You exalt the Lamb of God, not in part but in whole,

Endue me with power to plead for the heathen's soul;

Shine your light on sin's captives, whose hearts are darker than coal,

As on the day of Pentecost, come again, let us fulfill our Spirit-filled role.

CHAPTER 22

LET NO MAN SEIZE YOUR CROWN

"Who gave himself for us to redeem us from all lawlessness and to purify for himself a people for his own possession who are zealous for good works."

Titus 2:14

EVERY CHRISTIAN IS ASSIGNED A task which he is called to fulfill. We will remain alive and well amidst the turbulent journey until we are called home to Heaven. The final trumpet call is imminent for many, while the torrents of death will sweep some away and others will remain until the coming of the Lord. Nonetheless, we will all encounter the Lord. "For the Son of Man is going to come with his angels in the glory of his Father, and then he will repay each person according to what he has done'" (Matt. 16:27). Why is it that many Christians of our day that claim faith in the gospel are so far removed from the reality of the works of the gospel? While every other religion wears its works based on accomplishment as a necklace of pride, modern-day Christianity is clothed with a mere acknowledgment of faith that produces absolutely nothing. The time has come for you, oh Christian, to take up the call of evangelism and start knocking on your neighbor's door instead of waiting for them to knock at your door. If Mormons and Jehovah's Witnesses continue to multiply and spread across nations at an unforeseen rate to convert the unevangelized groups and, upon succession, turn the individual twice as much a child of Hell as themselves, where is the blush in the faces of our preachers and congregation that hold fast to every biblical doctrine while keeping it contained within the scopes of those who share the same worldview and never letting it see the light of day?

Were the Lord to remove His presence from our gatherings, I wonder how many would sense it? While many are constantly praying to be raptured from the coming Great Tribulation, the needed prayers are, in fact, for boldness and courage to enter the awful days that are ahead. God has given you a task; I beseech you to do it! Prayerlessness is a friend to laziness and laziness to sinfulness. I believe the only way to practice vigilance as a Christian is to stay in constant prayer. Sin is never too far from a slothful Christian. It is only a matter of time until the Christian gets entangled in its snare.

In the name of God's work, many church leaders are advancing their work. After all, everybody seems to have a vision these days. The vision involves making much of the planner's agenda veiled with spiritualized words of praise and God's affirmation; but in reality, it is craftily devised flattery at best. Listen, it is not a new vision that is needed today but obedience to the revealed mission of the Great Commission. If we have men and women in the Church who would endure some sleepless nights in prayer, there would be less money spent in accommodating man's vision and more power given to fulfilling the already laid down mission of evangelism derived from the Word of God.

While the workaholics of our society labor tirelessly to secure an easy and prosperous retirement plan for their distant future, with many of them at the cost of losing their health and well-being in the process, the Church stands idle and devoid of her duties to the world of lost sinners. She is sleeping comfortably in her past accomplishments, unwarily trading godly passion for worldly possessions in the present and heaping up excuses for her lack of obedience in the spread of the Great Commission. She will labor to preserve the citizenship of her home called Heaven but unmoved and without compassion when it comes to bringing souls to the Lord of her boasted home.

The world may reward your labor with a temporal crown of fleeting worth, whereas God will reward your labor with the eternal crown of unfading glory. Just look at what is at stake for Christians, who excuse themselves from the crucifixion of earthly pleasures and shun being awakened to the life of costly but rewarding service. One's missed opportunity is another's seized chance. In eternity, you will witness a fellow believer wearing a crown that you could have secured had it not been for your unceasing excuses for sacrificial obedience. Simply hearing the Word of God will not amount to any rewards, but applying the hearkened word is what secures Heavenly rewards. When God gives you a task to complete, do not cast it aside. Pursue it head-on unto completion. Christ's work is worth every drop of your blood, sweat, and tears, whereas the works of the flesh, with its blinding desires, are dead at the very roots. Every believer is called to obedience, regardless of race or social or financial status.

"But I discipline my body and keep it under control, lest after preaching to others I myself should be disqualified" (1 Cor. 9:27). Let every Christian, whether a preacher or a missionary, observe and preserve their spirituality through the ongoing practice of vigilance, especially in the area of bodily needs. Long hours of sleep and unrestricted indulgence in food have been one of the leading factors in plunging modern-day Christianity to spiritual unawareness of an all-time high. Most preachers are guilty of this; so, it is not shocking when the pew is corrupted with laziness. When preachers fail to lead by example, the pew will eventually run elsewhere for influence. Either we lead the pew by example or watch our pews be made an example of.

We have no shortage of professional, passionless, prayerless, and tearless preachers who have sold themselves to a life of self-preservation and preaching that takes away the offense of the cross, which appears to promote unity and peace. In reality, however, it is self-preservation under the cloak of wisdom and love—which is used in words only to avoid confrontations—and, last of all, inaction under the guise of practicing much caution. While we spend our saved souls on spiritual vacation, the enemy has already invaded our homes and institutions through the gates of our boasted liberties and taken many captives by the bait of additional comfort and security. The Lord will not tarry much longer, and the veil of deception that our churches have bought into will not hold up, especially with its exposure close at hand. "By whom?" you might ask, to which Heaven answers, by "the One who is high and lifted up, who inhabits eternity, whose name is Holy" (Isa. 57:15). Truly, the Lord is coming soon. Amen.

CHAPTER 23

HE IS WORTHY

"And I heard every creature in heaven and on earth and under the earth
and in the sea, and all that is in them, saying, 'To him who sits on the throne
and to the Lamb be blessing and honor and glory and might forever and ever.'"

Revelation 5:13

MY JOURNEY TO CHRISTIANITY BEGAN at the age of sixteen; and to this day, I get asked the question, "What made you convert to Christianity?" To which I respond, "It is not a method that drew me in, but the man, even the Lord Jesus Christ." It is He Who gave this insignificant dust a glorious reason to breathe. How could I have restrained myself from bowing my existence to the One Who "formed my inward parts" and "knitted me together in my mother's womb," from Whom "my frame was not hidden...when I was being made in secret, intricately woven in the depths of the earth"? How could I hide from the One who "fearfully and wonderfully" created me, whose "eyes saw my unformed substance," and written in His books were "the days that were formed for me when as yet there was none of them" (Psalm 139:13-16)? You do not need a Damascus-like conversion story, such as the apostle Paul's, to be an instrument of God's mercy. Nevertheless, a genuine conversion is essential, as one cannot offer mercy to others without first having experienced it oneself. The soul that encounters the mercy of God is compelled to seek it each day, as it cannot exist without this continual request.

I encourage the new converts to never let anyone talk them out of faith that defies creaturely logic and limitation, which, in essence, suppresses liberty for the Spirit's work, warranted in the name of carefulness. But by all means, exercise the faith of the Son of God while casting your soul in His care, for then you will undertake the sea of raging impossibility, causing the intellect to bow before the supernatural working of God. But Heaven would have you remember that holiness in the believer is the birthplace for all supernatural manifestations of God's power. And contrary to some denominational beliefs, it is not the manifestation of tongues that marks your spirituality. It is salvation unto holiness that stamps the seal of your conversion. I have stated this before and will do so again: salvation will never be gained by holiness but through faith alone. Holiness will be granted and pursued the moment you are regenerated. Church history itself bears witness to the acts of these holy men and women of God, who, despite their stumblings, have clothed many with the essence of true Christianity, fueled with the vision to see the Church ascend the hill of the Lord with clean hands and a pure heart.

After my arrival to the United States, I ran into a group of wonderful Christians who invited me to a weekly gathering at a house church. I attended the following week. After having witnessed the worshippers with tears of intercession running down their cheeks and songs of praise befriending the lips of desirous souls with united passion and appetite for intimacy with the Lord, I was left speechless. It was this spark that kindled my heart to seek inexpressible and speechless worship; and God, in His mercy, was already at work in bringing the desire to fruition.

In the coming days, months, and years, I would find myself in deep, prayerful meditations in the Word of God. Upon tirelessly surveying His worthiness from the foot of the cross, I labored to offer my purest love for the Lamb. Yet in that profound moment, I was made to realize the Lamb's journey to offer His deepest love for me. This was the revelation of all revelations to a soul that labored to win the love of God that was already won for him. Oh, the sweetest and loveliest picture of that love was revealed to me in our Lord's cup in Gethsemane when I realized that He drank my damnation to make me drink from the bowels of His mercy—the Father's cup of wrath, which He drank trembling on my behalf, so I could be made to drink the joy of His salvation. The Lord whose righteousness I despised and love I rejected had now enthroned my heart with His all-satisfying presence. He is worthy of having all my life and yours. If there is one thing that the cross proved to me, it is this: that God gave His all when He gave His only Son. Therefore, let us give our all to Him, who gave us His all. Anything less is not considered worship.

"He has told you, O man, what is good; and what does the LORD require of you but to do justice, and to love kindness, and to walk humbly with your God" (Micah 6:8)? We live in a world where injustice, envy, and arrogance dominate the societal structure and are unashamedly practiced. Had we men and women who put on justice like a robe, spread the sweet aroma of kindness, and were led with cords of humility, many by now would have been ushered into the kingdom of righteousness.

The neurologists and psychologists of our day are baffled by the scores of callers and patients flooding into their facilities in search of deliverance from what our professionals label as a mental disorder. They are then quickly diagnosed with certain medical terminology and are given numerous antidepressant medications. In the course of time, they become enslaved to the drug that promised them freedom and are bound with chains of addiction. I am in no way dismissing all mental cases within the following criteria, but how much of what gets thrown around as mental disability is simply a soul needing loving company? The only person who can lavish God's love on needy souls is no other than a Christian, in whose lips is the message of hope if he would but be moved with compassion enough to extend it.

I believe the cure for this generation's mental exhaustion will never be found in refilling the bottles of antidepressants but in fellowship with the person of Hope, namely the Lord Jesus Christ. Let us live and witness in such a way that sinners are unable to charge us of withholding the message of reconciliation on the Day of Judgment when, by all means, the door of evangelism lays wide open but, alas, the Christian's heart narrowly shut.

ABOUT THE AUTHOR

JASKA DUWADI WAS BORN IN Kathmandu, Nepal, where he lived for the first twelve years of his life. At the time, Nepal was experiencing a great political and economic crisis as a nation, leaving the masses without hope for a peaceful and assuring future. In his pursuit of enduring peace and a better education, Jaska left Nepal in 2008 and migrated to Sydney, Australia, with his family.

He continued his education in Sydney until 2009, when he moved to Adelaide, a city in southern Australia. While continuing his education, he was marvelously brought to faith in Jesus Christ in 2011. Three years later, he migrated to the United States to pursue a career as a personal trainer. Over the course of time, the call to ministry replaced his earthly passion and set him on a journey to pursue the Heavenly calling of preaching Christ crucified. He is now a founder of the Book of Remembrance Ministries and currently resides in Marshall, Virginia, with his wife and six children, and he is the pastor at Marshall Baptist Church.

Ambassador International's mission is to magnify the Lord Jesus Christ and promote His Gospel through the written word.

We believe through the publication of Christian literature, Jesus Christ and His Word will be exalted, believers will be strengthened in their walk with Him, and the lost will be directed to Jesus Christ as the only way of salvation.

For more information about
AMBASSADOR INTERNATIONAL
please visit:

www.ambassador-international.com

@AmbassadorIntl

www.facebook.com/AmbassadorIntl

Thank you for reading this book. Please consider leaving us a review on your social media, favorite retailer's website, Goodreads or Bookbub, or our website, and check out some of our other books on the following page.

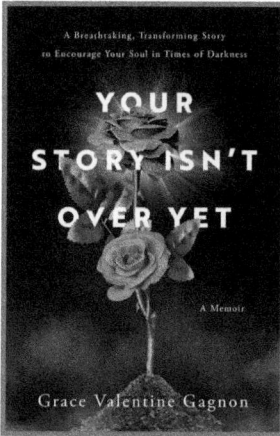

No matter how painful, dark, or challenging your situation is, you can have hope. *Your Story Isn't Over Yet* is a true story of how the sovereignty of God worked through the horrors of domestic violence, sexual assault, abortion, and trauma to ultimately show His unconditional love. Follow Grace's path of pain, loss, and perseverance to a pandemic love story and the joy that can be found only in Jesus.

When Jason Murfitt was a young man, he was confronted by his boss with the questions of how he knew what he believed were real. Like other men and women of faith, Jason was presented face-to-face with the living God, with undeniable evidence that led him to a desire to share the gospel with others. Join Jason as he looks at ten well-known men and women of faith who came to God in the most supernatural of ways. Jason presents the answers to many of the most commonly asked "whys" while intertwining them with personal testimonies from heroes in the faith.

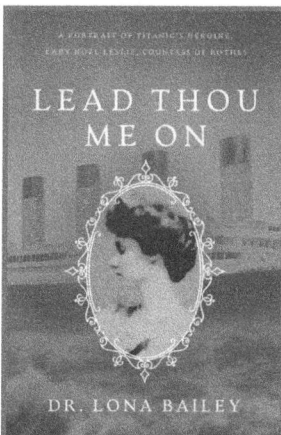

Britain's Lady Noël Leslie, Countess of Rothes, was one of the 325 first class passengers to board the Titanic on April 10, 1912. When the infamous disaster struck, Able Seaman Thomas Jones needed a second seaman to steer a lifeboat's tiller, and the Countess, with her pearls and fur coat under her life jacket, was chosen for the arduous job. The hymn "Lead Thou Me On" became much more than lyrics that night as the Countess relied on God to see fellow survivors to safety. Beyond the doomed voyage, Lady Noël had a fascinating and Christ-honoring life that is being told for the first time through this biography.

www.ingramcontent.com/pod-product-compliance
Lightning Source LLC
Chambersburg PA
CBHW071438090426
42737CB00011B/1696